AMERICAN INDUSTRY

KIM STEELE

AMERICAN INDUSTRY

Foreword by Paul Goldberger

ORO
ORO Editions — Novato, California

CONTENTS

FOREWORD
BY PAUL GOLDBERGER

Pulitzer Prize-winning architecture critic for *The New York Times*

There is something oddly reassuring about Kim Steele's photographs in *American Industry*, as if the "American century" had not passed, as if the manufacturing might of other nations had not risen to challenge American industrial power, as if digital technology had not made the conspicuous materiality of iron and steel less central to the economy than they once were. When you look at the images in this book the first association they bring, at least to my mind, is to the photographs of Charles Sheeler and Margaret Bourke-White, the greatest of the photographers who recorded American industrial power in the twentieth century. Kim Steele is surely the inheritor of their legacy, the photographer who carries their perceptions into the twenty-first century.

But to leave it at that is to misread him, to suggest that his photography is driven by nostalgia, and that his images are a conscious attempt to evoke another time. I don't think that is the case at all. While he continues the legacy of photographers like Sheeler and Bourke-White, and he, like them, sees beauty in what many fail to see as beautiful, he is no throwback, no denier of the present and its complexities. Too much of his subject matter is connected to our own time for that to be the case: the American industry that he photographs also includes atomic power, aeronautics, and space vehicles. And if you look at the full range of his work, the work that goes beyond the subject matter of this book, it cuts across the twenty-first century to touch on fashion, culture, nature, urbanism, technology, and people.

Much of this other work is in color, unlike the images in this book, which are all shot in black and white. He does this not to create a deliberate connection to his predecessors among photographers of industry. There is a much more important reason, I think, for his avoidance of color in these pages. Steele's great talent is as a photographer of patterns, and he shows us intricacy amidst boldness. These are images of monumentality and intimacy, dancing together. It's a dance both delicate and powerful, and color distracts from it. The patterns are clear in black and white. It makes us see what he is seeing.

This sense of pattern—which also recalls the majestic work of Paul Strand, as vital a predecessor as Sheeler and Bourke-White—is what leads Steele to photograph a steel skeleton rising on Madison Avenue in the midst of Manhattan, which he undoubtedly finds more interesting than the finished building. (In the case of the tower from the 1970s that he was shooting here, few would argue with him that the completed structure was less compelling than its framework.) What Steele is telling us here is that this huge and awesome thing, a skyscraper, is actually made up of a million smaller things that are not huge and not always awesome—beams and trusses and columns and bolts of steel that make patterns that will disappear when the building is complete, patterns that can be appealing in a way that finished facades are not. Louis Kahn once referred to a famous postwar glass tower as "a beautiful lady in hidden corsets" because its skeleton, like that of most skyscrapers, was hidden, and you sense that Steele would agree. He wants to show us the corsets. But this image is also about process, since the photographer has frozen time so that we can see the building's innards, the innards that by necessity become invisible within the completed enormity of the tower. Here, they become the composition of his photograph.

The skyscraper image is unusual among these pictures, however, since it is one of the few that hints at a broader context: most of Steele's images of industrial might take us only inside the thing itself and pay no heed to the place in which it is set. All the better to show us the patterns that Steele inevitably finds, the combinations of line, mass, and shadow to create a whole other kind of picture that is separate from the subject of the photograph, a thing that Steele's eye finds embedded in that thing that is his subject.

And yet the patterns, clear as they are, never dominate: the photograph is never only or even predominantly about the pattern, but about its subject first and foremost. If these images serve to remind us that photography is inevitably an art of composition and that Steele is a fine compositionalist, his instinct to show us patterns never gets to the point where the entire image becomes purely an abstraction, disconnected from the thing that is its subject. The telescope is still a telescope, the turbine is still a turbine, the dam is still a dam, whatever the pattern of lines and solids and voids that Steele's eye makes us see within it.

These are machines, machines that exist to serve and that normally are in the background of our consciousness, or out of our field of vision entirely. Steele puts them in the foreground, makes us focus on their beauty as objects, on their clarity—another reason it is good that these images are all in black and white, since it enhances the crispness and clearness that is a key part of what he is seeing. These photographs are about precision, and you feel that Steele owes his subjects precision because precision is key to every one of the things he is shooting. To be imprecise would, in a way, dishonor the industrial power that he is celebrating.

When you look at these images you also feel the materials—the glimmer of metal most of all, but sometimes its opacity and solidity, and also the coolness and depth of concrete, and the pliability of rubber, with wires swirling in rhythmic syncopation. You feel weight, too, in these pictures—the weight of great, solid physical masses—but you also feel space, and objects set within it. Steele is ruminating about permanence here, about not only enormous physical presence but about the idea of things made to last, which is how he views everything he shows us here, which is why this book is, among other things, a photographer's essay on monumentality.

But perhaps what you feel most of all is the potential of movement; even though everything he photographs is at rest, you are aware that the aircraft fuselage can begin to move through space, that the cylinders in the engine will begin to turn, or that water will cascade through the opening in the dam. These are objects that have the power to do things that this photography does not show us. What it does instead is something more subtle: it fills us with an awareness of the pent-up energy that lies within every one of these objects. It seems altogether natural to learn that Kim Steele is the son of a fighter pilot and grew up amid powerful jet planes. Like every talented son who is influenced by his father, he both followed him and broke away to make his own turf. He translated his father's world of fighter jets into a broader interest in monumentality and American industrial power; none of these pictures are about flight itself. But in every one of them you can feel the son's excitement about his father's world, transformed into his own art.

East Hampton, New York, 2020

ARTIST STATEMENT
BY KIM STEELE

I was fortunate to pursue my passion during the last golden age of photography—the 1980s in New York when rent was still reasonable and commercial work booming. Corporations had lavish magazines, and newspapers and print media were flourishing. I arrived at the right time and hit the ground running, found a raw loft on lower Broadway, and published in *Life Magazine* within a year. I fell into the crowd at Andy Warhol's Factory, and went clubbing at AREA with Basquiat, Futura, and Haring when FUN Gallery was ruling. I exhibited my industrial landscapes, in large-format black-and-white prints, at OK Harris Gallery, and began to exhibit in museums, be included in corporate collections, and be acquired by the likes of MoMA, SFMOMA, Goldman Sachs, Exxon, and Seagram's.

Relationship between form and function has always fascinated me. Turning structure into form has been my goal for almost forty years. Fascinated by architecture, as well as industry, I am ever drawn to capture their form and convert them to shapes bespeaking their power and strength. I enjoy experiencing these spaces—the magnitude of a dam looming over me or the crackling of electricity all around me. The locations are intoxicating. When trying to convert an inanimate object—a laser exciter, aircraft, shipping infrastructure, steel, nuclear plants, atomic energy, accelerators, space, and satellites—to portend its meaning, like fusion, then I feel alive. The power and muscularity also draw me to these locations—embodying an American Dream.

To shoot new technology on film, with my ancient Hasselblad, was exciting. The camera parallels the materials that I have been shooting for thirty years—metal in its various forms. With this new technology, analog provides a rich contrast with digital photography, since there is so much data in our current world. The silver in the film echoes the materials being shot. I understand the organic nature of film and over the years have learned to appreciate its unique properties.

The same form resides in the twenty-first century that I had explored in the last century, but absent the steel mills and coal trains. This century differs from the last in terms of "American Might." America ruled almost every area of industry—steel, aviation, shipbuilding—but the current times focus is on technology as seen in these photographs: a machine the size of a 737 that zaps cancerous tumors; a robot that assists disabled people to walk again and lead a more normal life; or our astrophysicist's drive to find the origins of the universe and its most fundamental elements. These monstrous new machines are focused on very small particles, but their scale and significance is revealed in these images.

San Francisco, May 2022

AVIATION

NOSE

Boeing Plant, Everett, Washington
1979

This photo captures the iconic power of the Boeing 747 nose. One of its most unique features, the Boeing 747 can open its nose to load freight. The 747 is the result of the work of 50,000 Boeing employees, “the Incredibles.” Boeing set out to develop a large advanced commercial airplane to take advantage of the high-bypass engine technology developed for the C-5A. The tail of the 747 is as tall as a six-story building. Pressurized, it carried a ton of air and had room for 3,400 pieces of baggage. The 747-8I, the current passenger variant in production, is capable of carrying 467 passengers in a typical 3-class configuration, has a range of 8,000 miles, and a cruising speed of 570 mph. The total wing area is larger than a basketball court. The entire global navigation system weighs less than a modern laptop computer. The Boeing Everett factory was designed and built to accommodate the assembly of these large planes (23 at one time). Boeing announced the end of production of this mighty craft’s last legacy, the Boeing 747-8, in 2020.

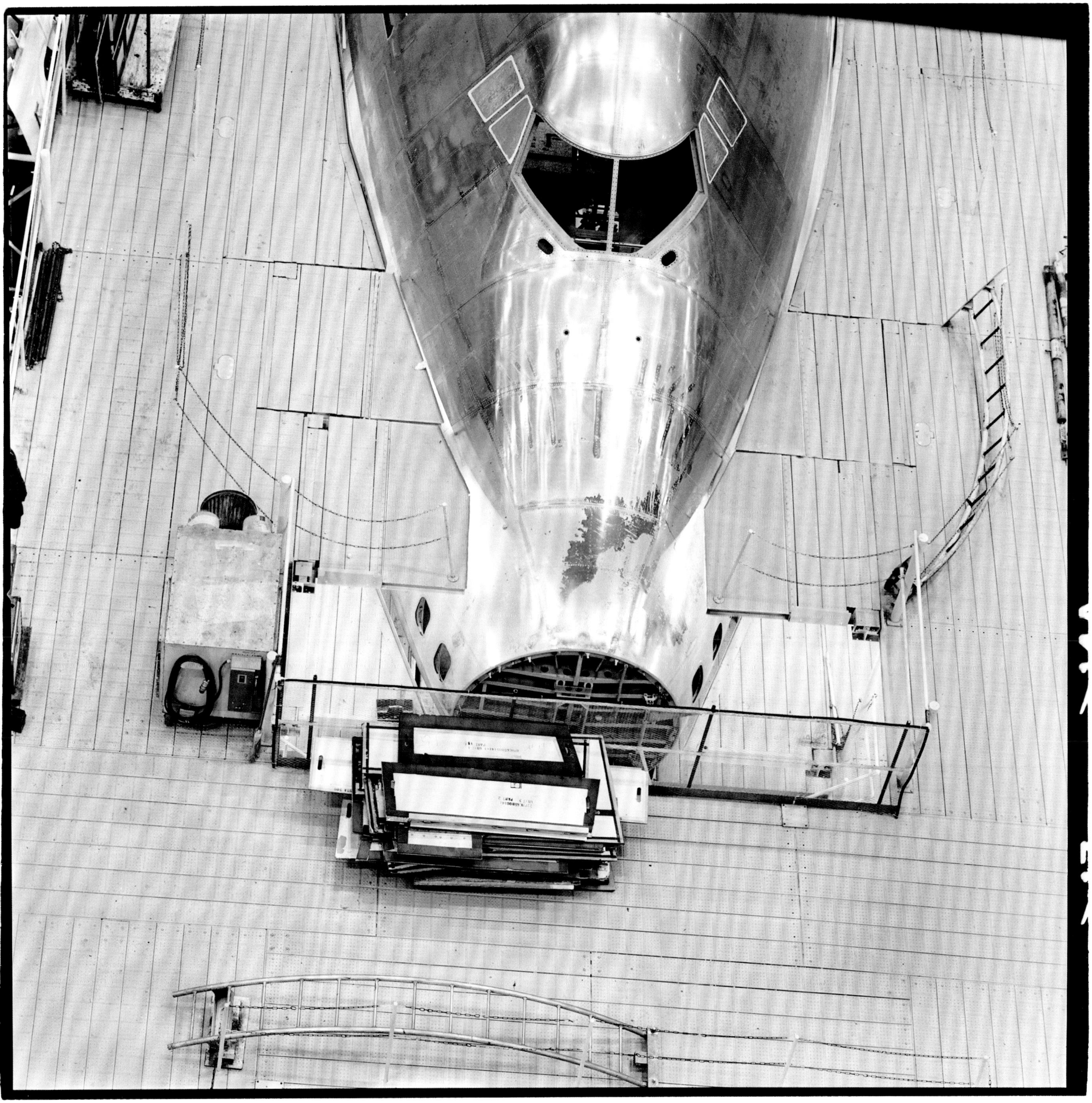

METROPOLIS

Boeing Plant, Everett, Washington
1978

This image was titled after the Fritz Lang film of the same title. The Boeing Plant in Everett is the world's largest room, with three floors. Plans for the factory were first announced in 1966, for the construction of twenty-five 747s for Pan American World Airways. During peak production years, every shift had 10,000 workers, three shifts each day. The Everett factory has a fleet of 1,300 bicycles on hand to help cut travel time. It has its own fire station and medical services. Overhead, a multitude of cranes are used to move the heavier aircraft parts, as the planes take shape. In summer, if it gets too hot, they open the massive doors to let in the breeze. In winter, the effect of one million lights, the huge amount of electric equipment, and 10,000 human bodies helps moderate the temperatures. There is a longstanding urban myth that the building is so large it creates its own weather system, and that clouds form overhead. By June 2019, 1,554 aircraft had been built, with twenty 747-8s remaining on order.

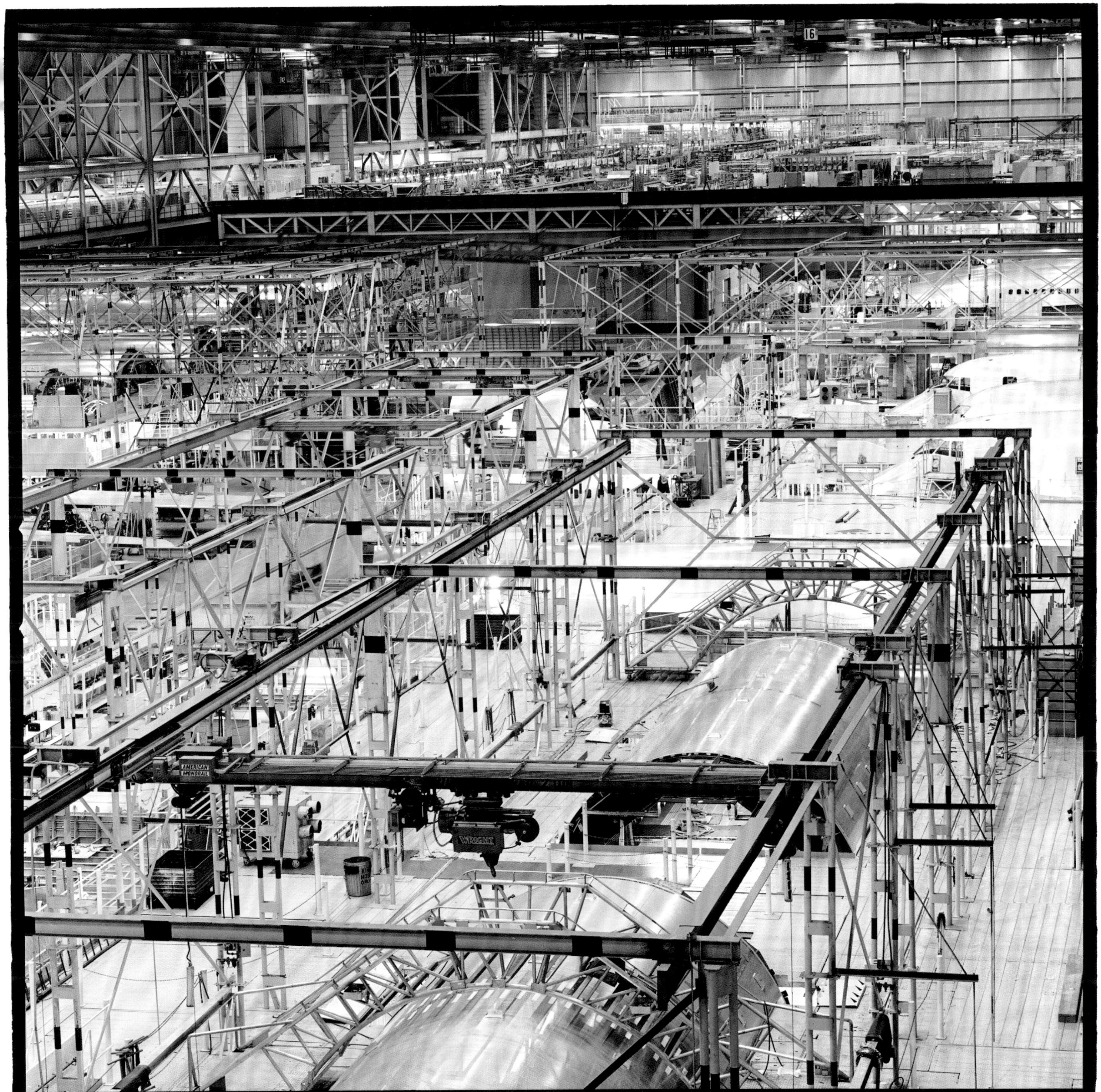
16
AMERICAN
MONORAIL
WRIGHT

INFRASTRUCTURE

Boeing Plant, Everett,
Washington
1978

Designer Joe Sutter left the 737 development team to design the 747. The Boeing 747 was ultimately made possible through new engine technology. One of the main enablers that made such a larger aircraft possible was the advent of high bypass turbofan engines, which delivered twice the power of turbojets that were in use at the time, and used one third less fuel. General Electric had applied the principle to the C5 Galaxy project. Pratt & Whitney was also working on this concept, and in 1966 Pan American, Boeing, and Pratt & Whitney agreed to develop the JT9D as the powerhouse engine for the 747. Arguably one of the most recognizable aircraft in the skies, the Boeing 747, also known as the Jumbo Jet or Queen of the Skies, reigned supreme as the largest flying commercial airliner until the introduction of the Airbus A380, now discontinued. On September 30, 1968, the first 747 was rolled out. With ten-abreast economy seating, it typically accommodates 366 passengers in three travel classes.

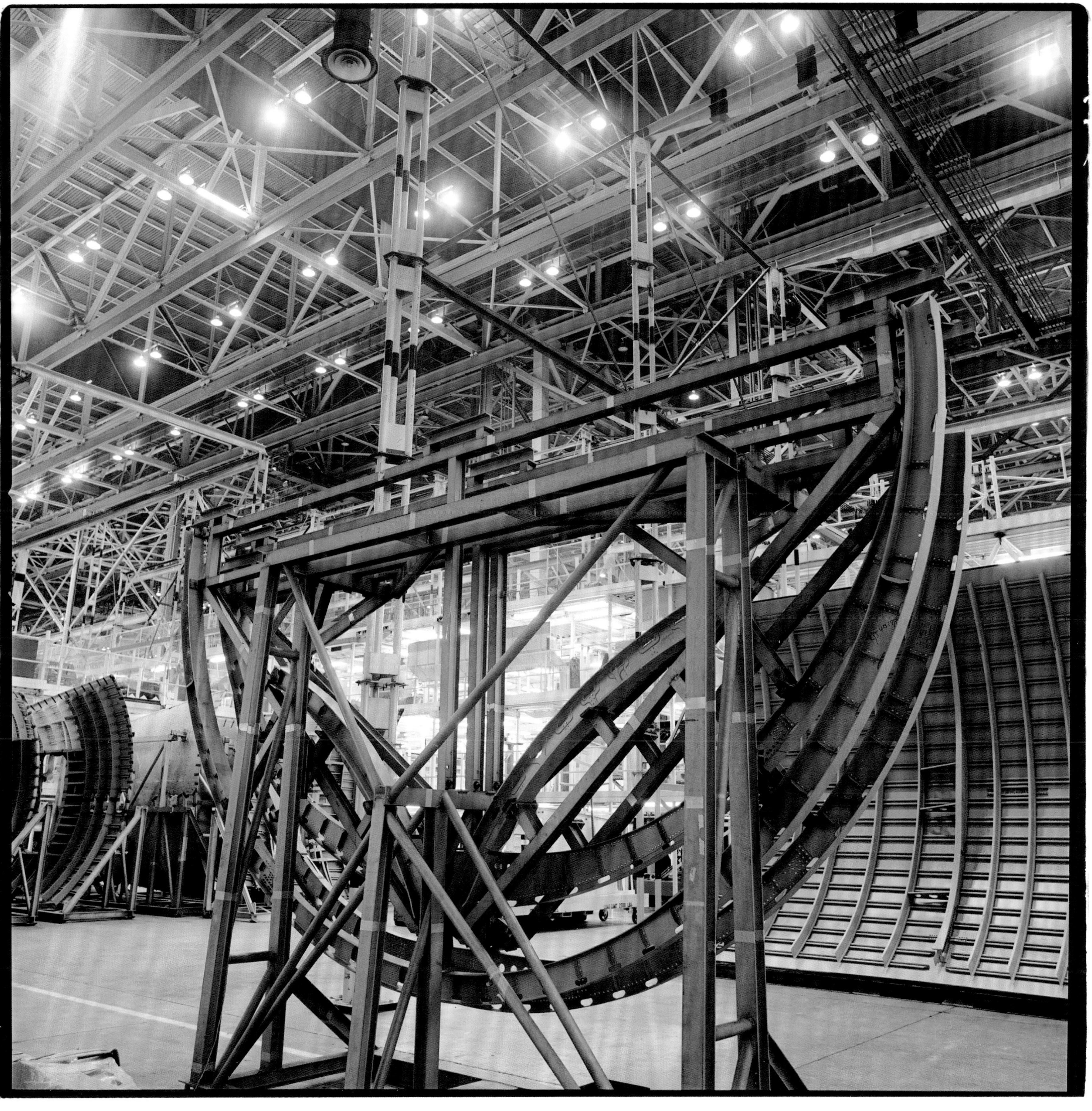

APACHE NOSE

Army attack helicopter,
Fort Rucker, Alabama
1985

The Boeing AH-64, Apache—its predecessor the Cobra—is an American twin-turboshaft attack helicopter with a tailwheel-type landing gear arrangement and a tandem cockpit for a crew of two. It features a nose-mounted sensor suite for target acquisition and night vision systems. It is armed with a 30mm M230 chain gun carried between the main landing gear, under the aircraft's forward fuselage, and four hardpoints mounted on stub-wing pylons for carrying armament and stores, AGM-114 Hellfire missiles, and Hydra 70 rocket pods first developed by Hughes Helicopters. Highly maneuverable and heavily armed, the combat-proven Apache helicopter is the backbone of the US Army's all-weather, ground-support capability. In 1984, it was purchased by McDonnell Douglas, who continued production, and was ultimately purchased by Boeing. To date, 2,400 helicopters have been produced. Boeing has sold them to Greece, Israel, Japan, the UAE, and the UK, to name just a few of the countries using the Apache.

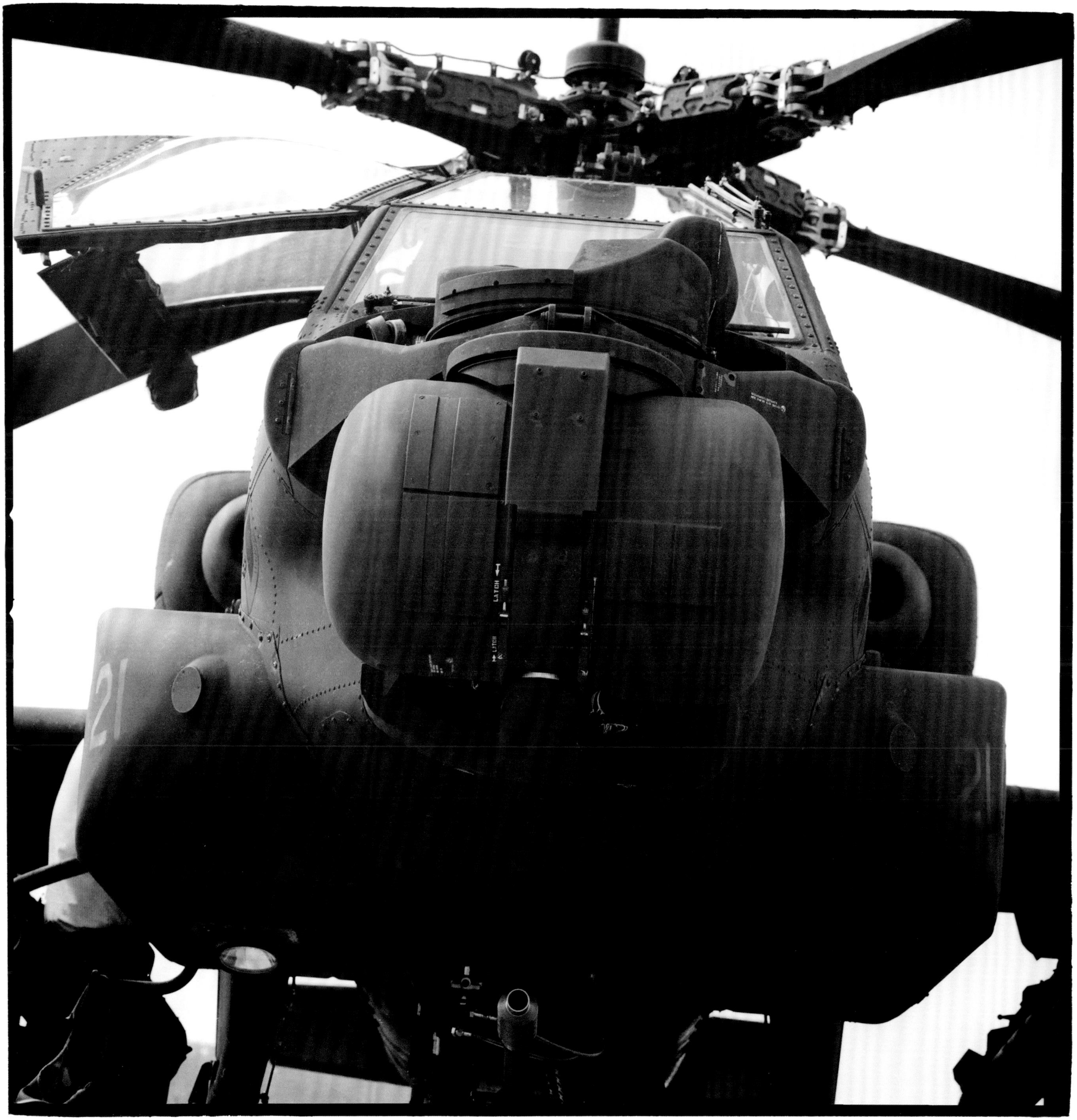
21
LATCH
LATCH

SUPERCOBRA

US Marine attack helicopter,
Fort Worth, Texas
1986

The Bell AH-1 SuperCobra is a twin-engine attack helicopter based on the United States Army's single-engine AH-1 Cobra. The twin Cobra family, itself part of the larger Huey family, includes the AH-1J SeaCobra, the AH-1T Improved SeaCobra, and the AH-1W SuperCobra. The AH-1W, the backbone of the United States Marine Corps' attack helicopter fleet for decades, is being replaced by the next generation Bell AH-1Z Viper. The AH-1J also received a more powerful gun turret. It featured a three barrel 20 mm XM197 cannon that was based on the six barrel M61 Vulcan cannon. The AH-1Z's two redesigned wing stubs are longer, each with a wingtip station for a missile, such as the AIM-9 Sidewinder, whose fly-by-wire design is guided by the laser viewer of the pilot. Its width is slightly more than the pilot's shoulders. To date, some 1,270 models have been produced for the United States Marines, and the armies of Iran, South Korea, and Turkey.

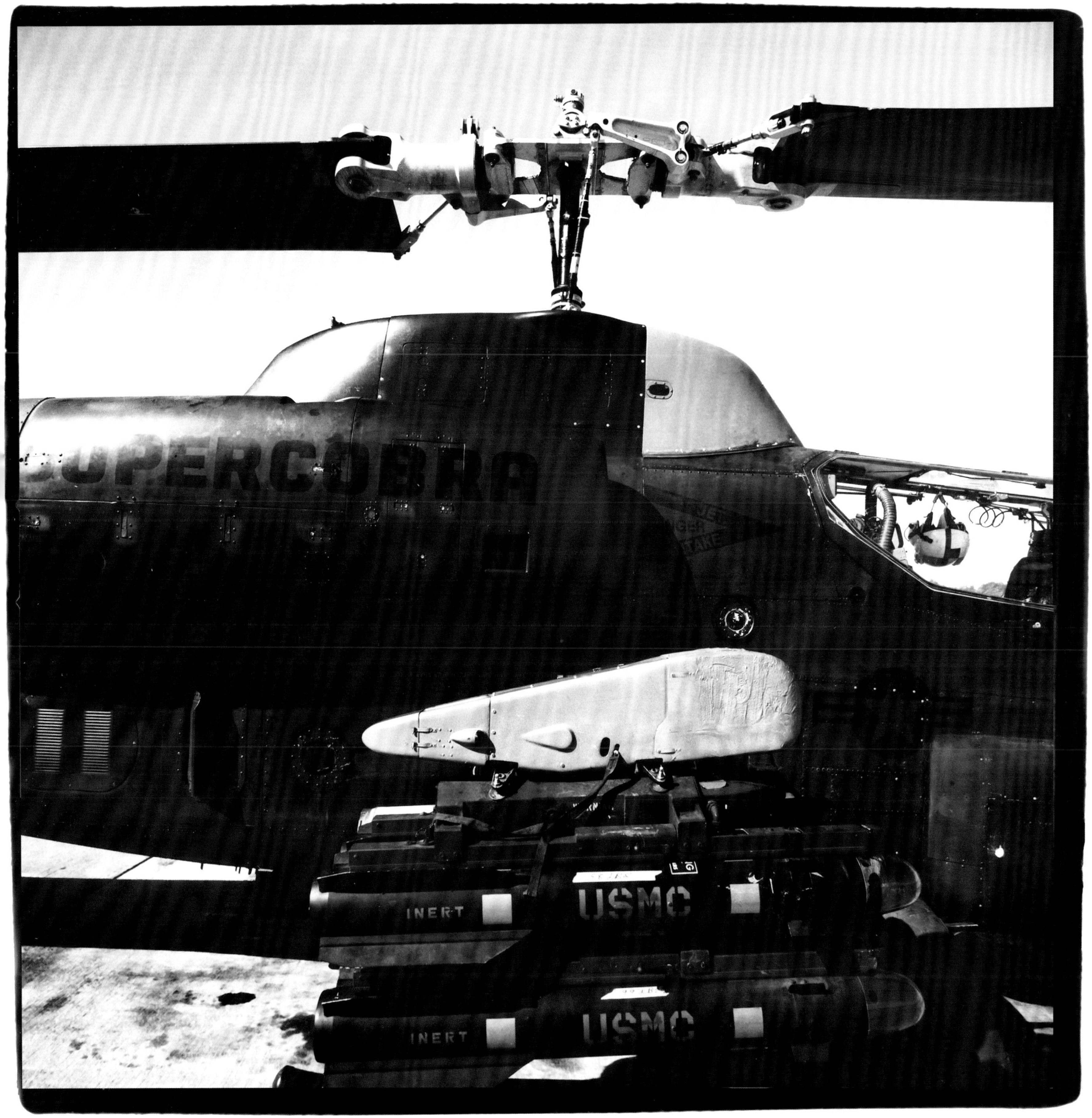
INERT
USMC
INERT
USMC

SUPER STALLION

Heavy-lift cargo helicopter, CH-53A,
Sikorsky Plant, Connecticut
1987

The CH-53 was the product of the US Marine Corps' "Heavy Helicopter Experimental" (HH(X)) competition, begun in 1962. The Sikorsky CH-53 Super Stallion heavy-lift helicopter first flew in 1974, and entered service with the US Marine Corps in 1981. A total of 172 Super Stallions have been delivered, with 165 in service with Marine Corps squadrons in the Pacific and Atlantic fleets. The Marine Corps uses the Super Stallion in the amphibious assault role and for transporting heavy equipment. The US Navy also uses the Super Stallion for vertical delivery and recovery of damaged aircraft on aircraft carriers. In 2000, the USMC announced the CH-53X program would extend its service life to 2025. The Super Stallion fuselage is watertight and constructed of light alloy steel and titanium. The helicopter is equipped with a Hamilton Sundstrand automatic flight control system, with two digital flight control computers, a four-axis auto-pilot, an attitude and heading reference system, a Rockwell Collins global positioning system, and a Northrop Grumman Doppler radar. The helicopter night vision system allows low-altitude operations at night and in adverse weather. The CH-53A is equipped with two T64-GE 6 turboshaft engines, with a maximum gross weight of 46,000 pounds.

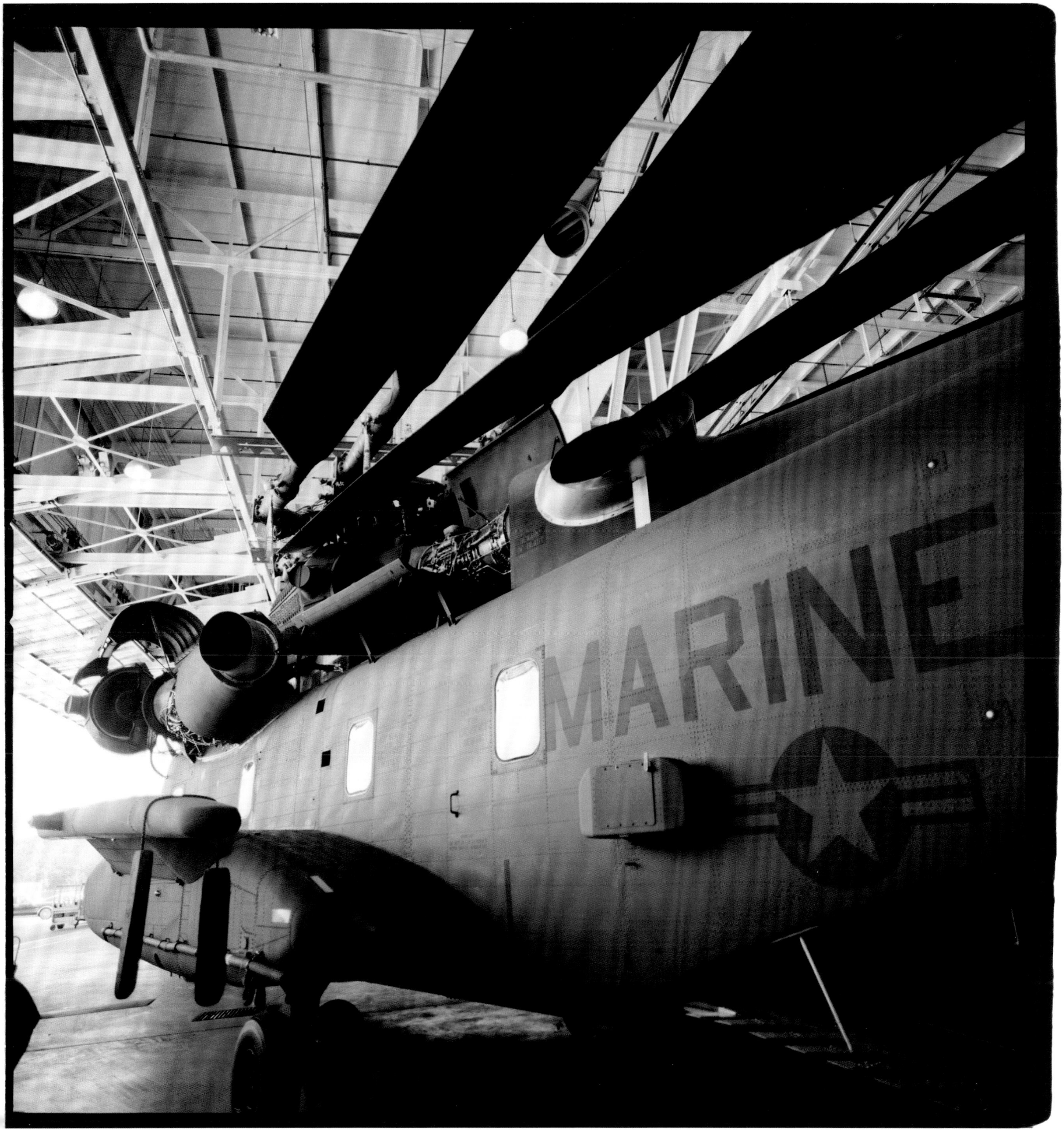
MARINE

B-1 BOMBER NOSE

In anechoic chamber testing the avionics,
Raytheon in Lexington, Massachusetts
1993

Built by Rockwell, and now Boeing, the Lancer is a supersonic variable-sweep wing, heavy bomber used by the United States Air Force. It is commonly called the "Bone" (from B-One). It is one of three strategic bombers in the US Air Force fleet as of 2020, the other two being the B-2 Spirit and the B-52 Stratofortress. This version had a top speed of Mach 2.2 at high altitude and the capability of flying for long distances at Mach 0.85 at low altitudes. Carrying the largest conventional payload of both guided and unguided weapons in the Air Force inventory, the multi-mission B-1B is the backbone of the United States' long-range bomber force. The B-1B's blended wing/body configuration, variable-geometry wings, and turbofan afterburning engines combine to provide long range, maneuverability, and high speed while enhancing survivability. The B-1B holds almost 50 world records for speed, payload, range, and time of climb in its class. The Air Force had 62 B-1Bs in service as of 2016. The B-1B is expected to continue to serve into the 2030s, with the Northrop Grumman B-21 Raider to begin replacing the B-1B after 2025. The B-1s in inventory are planned to be retired by 2036.

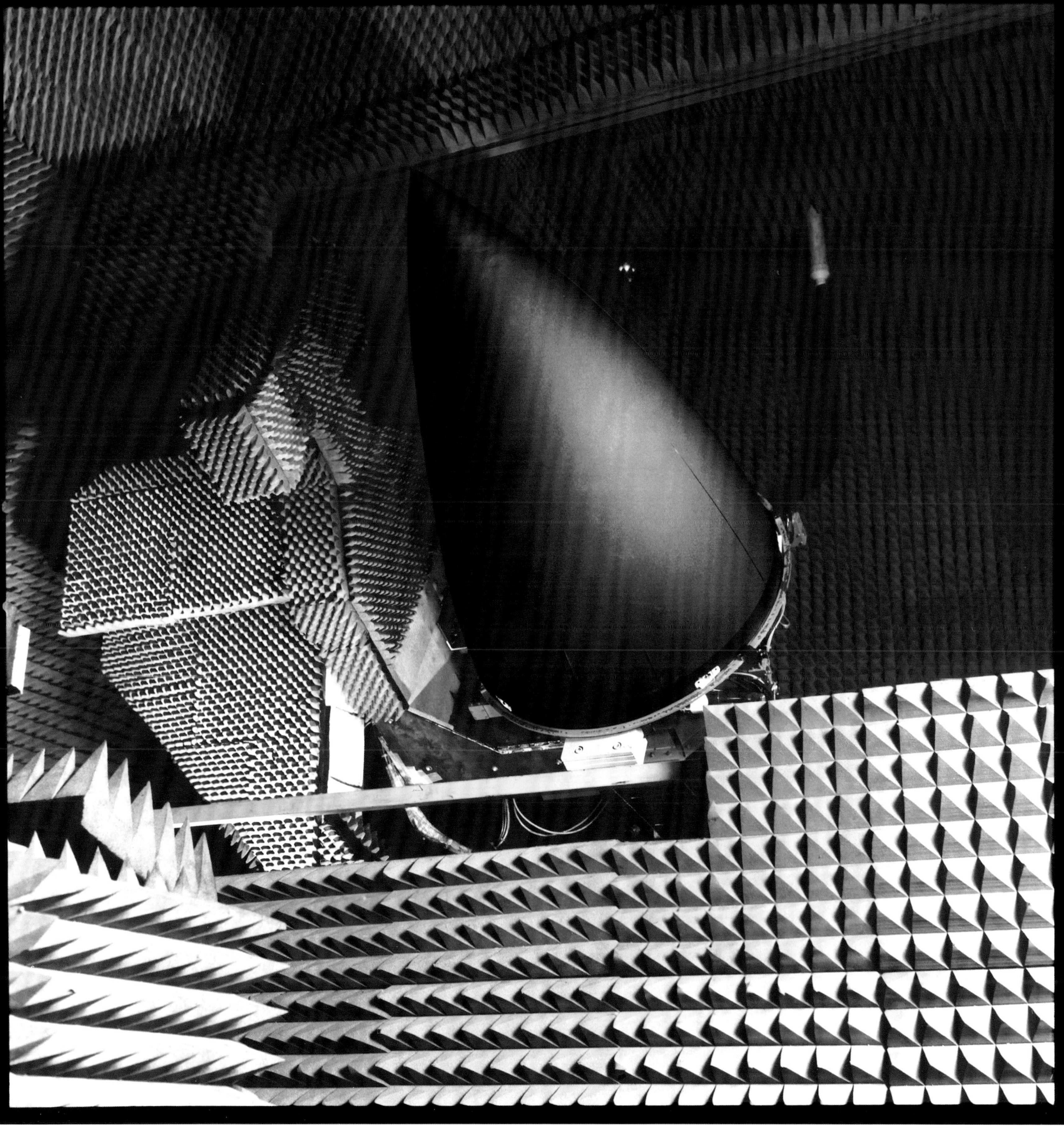

F-16 FIGHTING FALCON JET

Nellis Air Force Base, Nevada
1988

The General Dynamics F-16 Fighting Falcon is a single-engine, supersonic, multirole fighter aircraft originally developed by General Dynamics for the United States Air Force. Designed as an air superiority day fighter, it evolved into a successful all-weather multirole aircraft. Over 4,600 aircraft have been built since production was approved in 1976. This is the same aircraft employed by the Air Force Thunderbirds. The F-16 is highly maneuverable and has proven itself in air-to-air combat and air-to-surface attack. In an air combat role, the F-16's maneuverability and combat radius exceed that of all potential fighter aircraft threats. It can locate targets in all weather conditions and detect low-flying aircraft in radar ground clutter. In an air-to-surface role, the F-16 can fly more than 500 miles, deliver its weapons with superior accuracy, defend itself against enemy aircraft, and return to its starting point. The F-16 was designed by a consortium: the United States, Belgium, Denmark, the Netherlands, and Norway. The F-16 has an internal M61 Vulcan cannon. The Falcon 1 suite includes a wide-angle HUD that can display FLIR imagery, the Striker Helmet-Mounted Display (HMD), a datalink capability, and the FIAR *Grifo* radar.

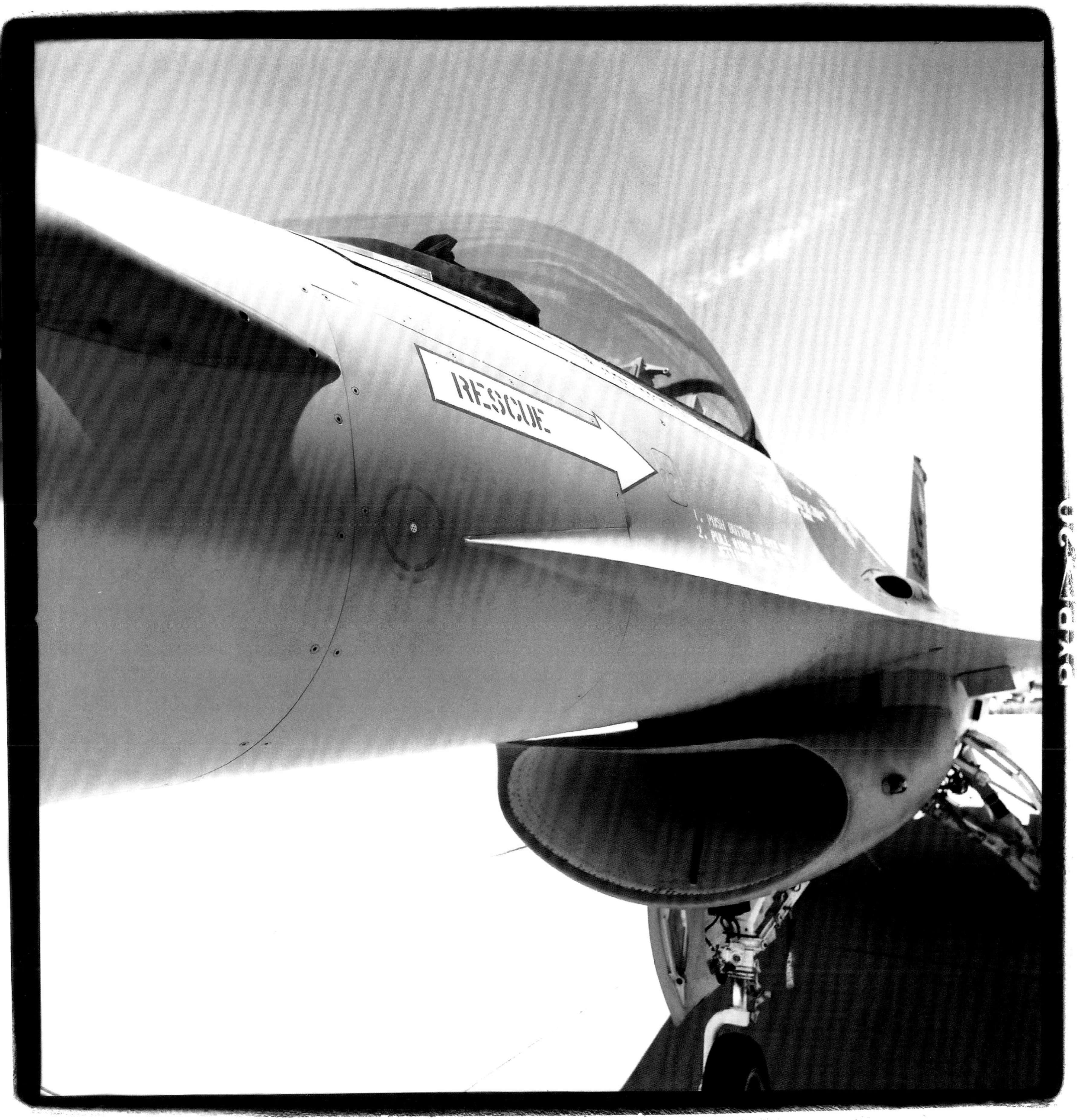
RESCUE

PRATT & WHITNEY GTF ENGINE

East Hartford, Connecticut
1990

The GTF engine, with its revolutionary geared fan, transformed aviation by delivering game-changing economic and environmental performance. The idea of a geared turbofan engine centers on the principle of a bypass ratio. Modern turbofan engines produce thrust in two manners: first, there are the compressors and combustion chamber at its core, and second, the fan at the front, which is driven by the jet core and directs air through bypass compartments around the core of the engine. The bypass ratio is the proportion of the air that bypasses the core versus the amount that goes through it. A higher bypass ratio means quieter, more efficient, and more powerful engines. This engine also incorporates advances in aerodynamics, lightweight materials, and other major technological improvements in the high-pressure spool, low-pressure turbine, combustor, controls, and engine health monitoring. The GTF engine powers five aircraft platforms: Airbus A220, the Airbus A320neo family, and Embraer E190-E2 already in commercial service. The engine's success is unique in the history of aircraft propulsion. With its sensors, the GTF generates approximately 4 million data points per engine per flight, or 1.02 terabytes of data per second.

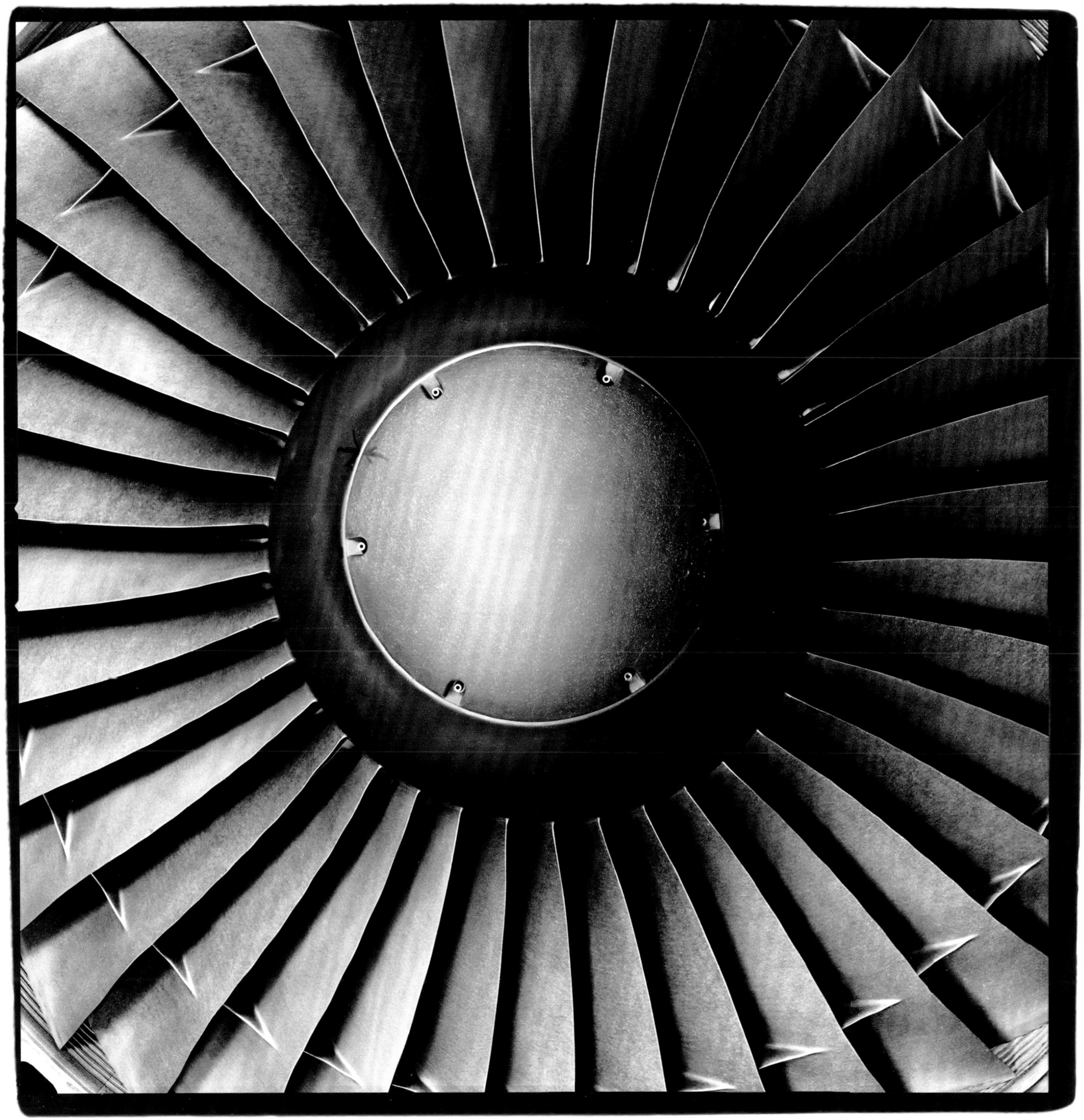

DIRIGIBLE

Akron, Ohio
1986
Courtesy: LIFE Magazine

The Goodyear Blimp is one of a fleet of airships, or dirigibles, operated by the Goodyear Tire and Rubber Company, used mainly for advertising purposes and capturing aerial views of live sporting events for television. From the launch of the *Pilgrim* in 1925 to the retiring of the *Spirit of Innovation* in 2017, Goodyear generally owned and operated non-rigid airships in its global public relations fleet. The term blimp itself is defined as a non-rigid airship—without any internal structure, the pressure of lifting gas contained within the airship envelope maintains the vessel's shape. The usual gases used for lifting airships are hydrogen and helium. Hydrogen is the lightest known gas and thus has great lifting capacity, but it is also highly flammable and has caused many fatal airship disasters, most notably the *Hindenburg* in Lakehurst, NJ, in 1937, which ended the effort to transport passengers by dirigibles. Helium is not as buoyant, but is far safer than hydrogen because it does not burn. The gas-containing envelopes of early airships used cotton fabric impregnated with rubber, a combination that was eventually superseded by synthetic fabrics such as neoprene and Dacron. Although technically incorrect, Goodyear continues to use "blimp" in reference to its new semi-rigid dirigibles.

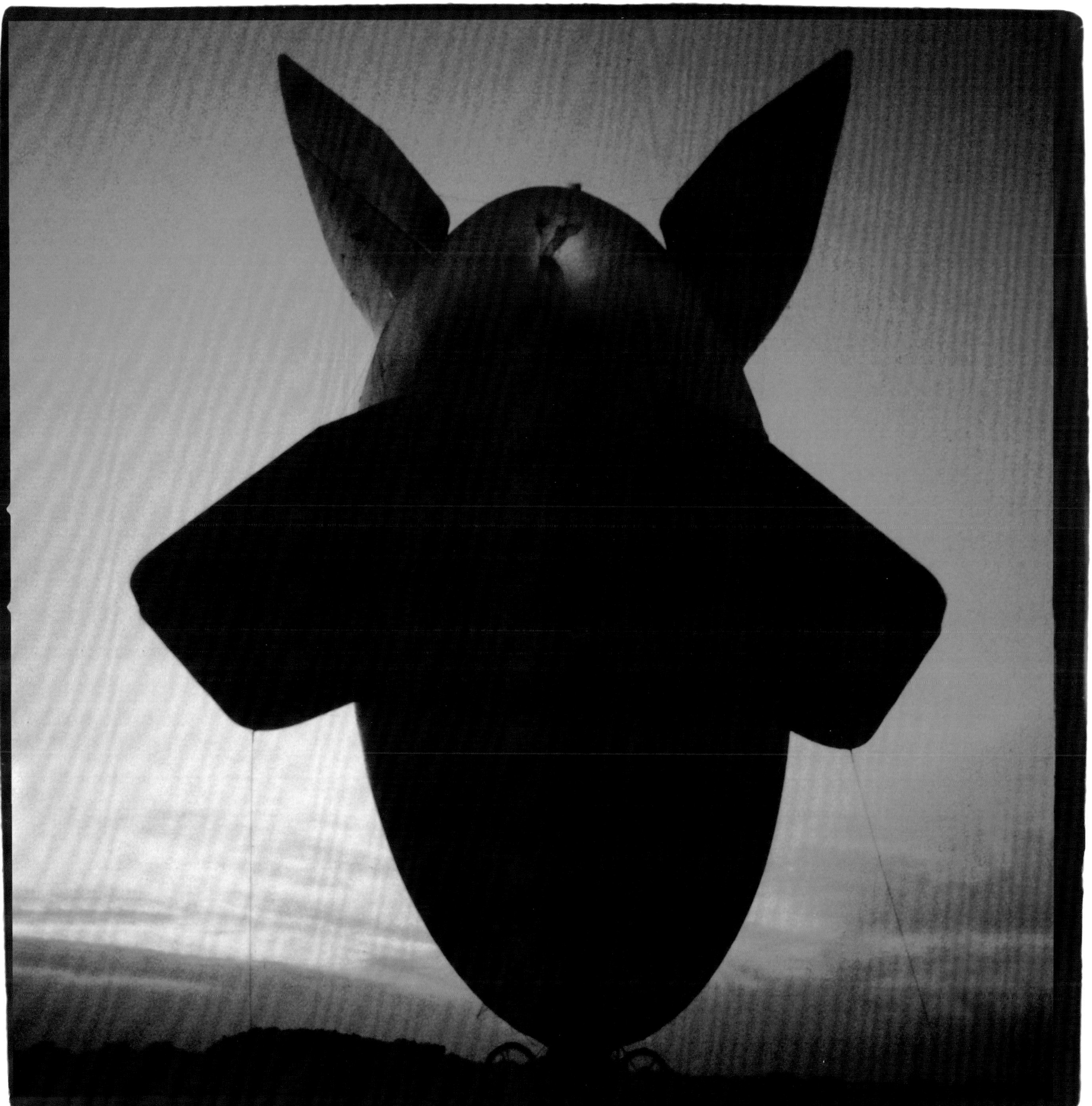

ATOMS

COCKROFT-WALTON

Fermilab, Chicago, Illinois
1985

The Cockcroft-Walton generator was developed at the University of Cambridge in the early 1930s to accomplish the first artificial splitting of the atom. Established in 1967 at Fermilab, the Cockroft-Walton propels the beam of protons around the four-mile circular track, bent by magnets, to collide in order to analyze the sub-particle compositions. The generator, or multiplier, is an electric circuit that generates a high DC voltage from a low-voltage AC input. Physicists John Douglas Cockcroft and Ernest Thomas Sinton Walton used this circuit design in 1932, to initially power their particle accelerator, performing the first artificial nuclear disintegration in history, which, in 1951, won them the Nobel Prize in Physics. Fermilab is America's first particle physics and accelerator laboratory. The inventor, Enrico Fermi, was an Italian physicist and the creator of the world's first nuclear reactor, the Chicago Pile-1. Fermi is called the "architect of the nuclear age," and the "architect of the atomic bomb." He was awarded the 1938 Nobel Prize in Physics for his work on "induced radioactivity by neutron bombardment," and for the discovery of trans-uranium elements. At Fermilab, they also probe the farthest reaches of the universe, seeking out dark matter and dark energy, which comprise 95% of the universe.

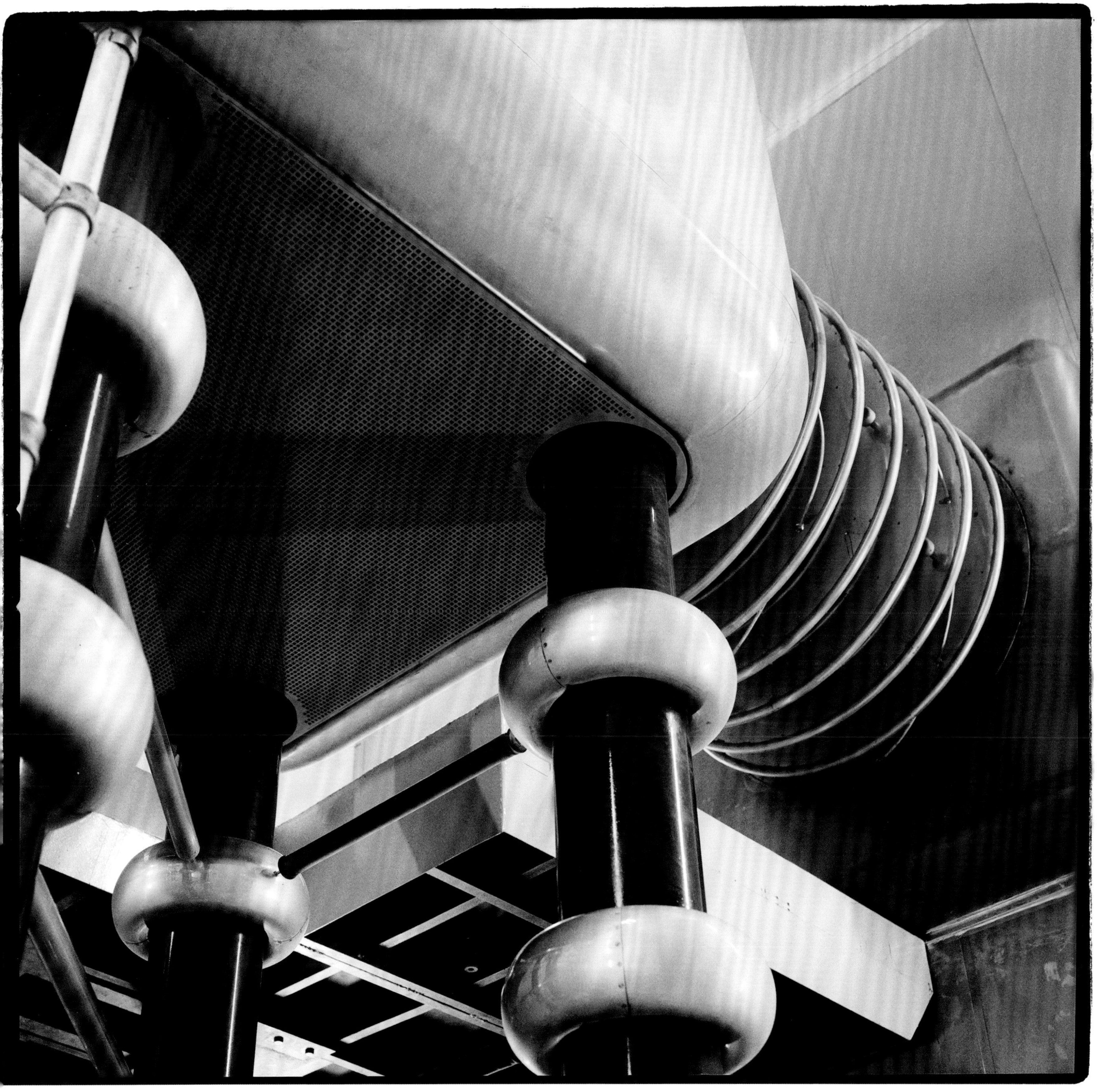

RINGS

Fermilab, Chicago, Illinois
1985

This photograph captures Fermilab's Main Ring, the laboratory's original particle accelerator, used for experiments that advanced our understanding of the ultimate structure of sub-matter, the standard model of particle interactions. Fermilab was the only facility, before CERN, to produce evidence of the last of the quarks, the top quark. The protons coming from the linear accelerator travel around the booster 20,000 times in 33 milliseconds. In 1969, physicist Robert Wilson directed construction of Fermilab's Main Ring. In 1972, the first beam of 200-billion-electron-volt protons circled its four-mile circumference, and the Main Ring reached its operating energy of 400 billion electron volts. In 1977, physicist Leon Lederman used the accelerator's particle beams to reveal the bottom quark, the first quark of the third generation of elementary particles that are nature's ultimate building blocks. Since 1983, the Main Ring has served as an injector to the Tevatron, where in 1995, physicists discovered the top quark, in collisions between protons and antiprotons, their antimatter counterparts. This is the most powerful proton-antiproton collider designed to reach one TeV.

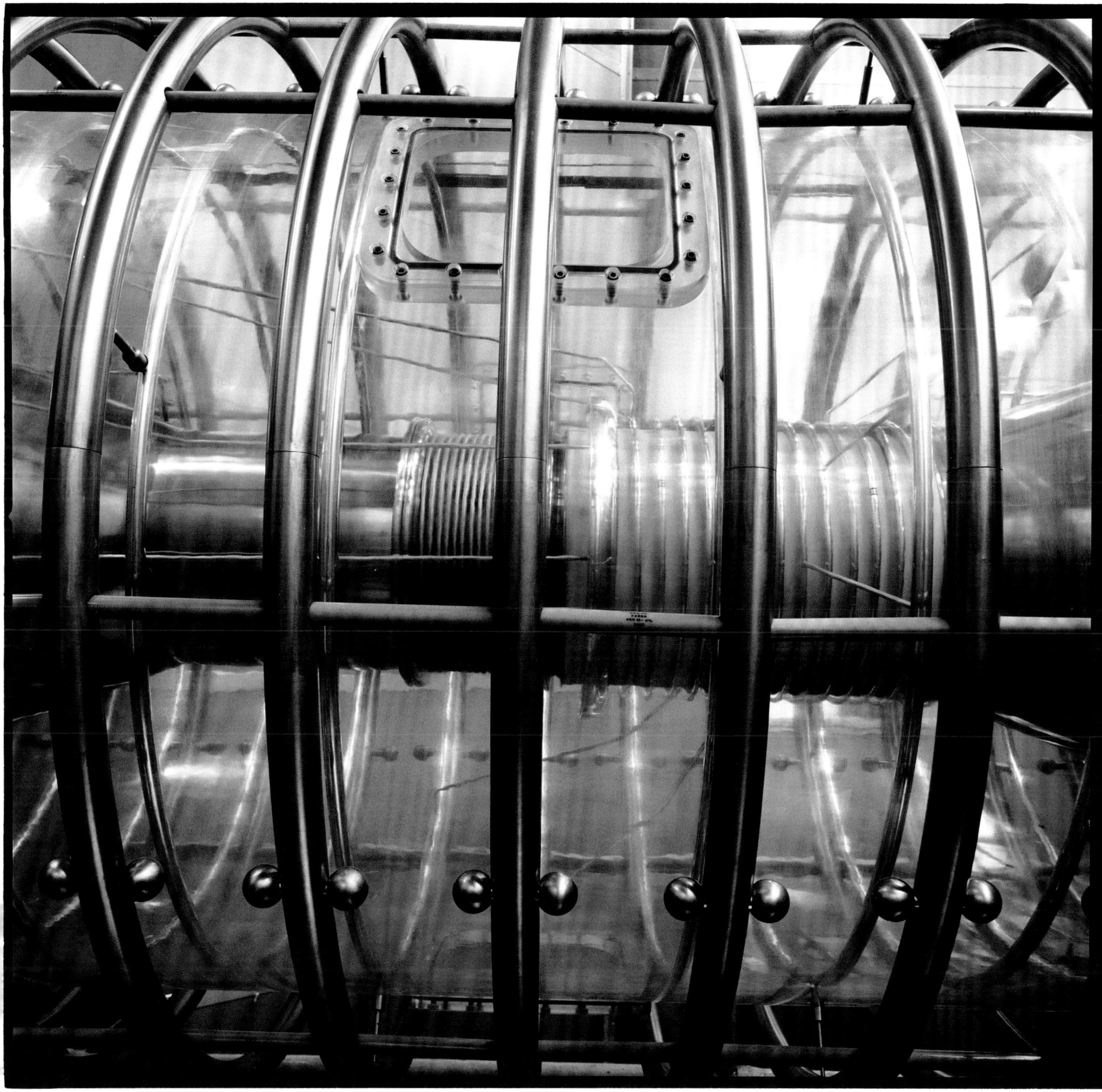

SHIVA

Laser Fusion, Lawrence Livermore Laboratory, California
1986

The Shiva laser, about the size of a football field, is a powerful 20-beam infrared neodymium glass laser built at Lawrence Livermore National Laboratory in 1977, for the study of inertial confinement fusion (ICF) and long-scale-length laser-plasma interactions. The basic idea of any ICF device is to rapidly heat the outer layers of a "target," normally a small plastic sphere containing a few milligrams of fusion fuel, typically a mix of deuterium and tritium. The heat burns the plastic into plasma, which explodes off the surface. Due to Newton's third law, the remaining portion of the target is driven inwards, eventually collapsing into a small point of very high density. The rapid blowoff also creates a shock wave that travels toward the center of the compressed fuel. When it meets itself in the center of the fuel, the energy in the shock wave further heats and compresses the tiny volume around it. If the temperature and density of that small spot is raised high enough, fusion reactions will occur. Shiva delivered more than ten kilowatts of energy in less than a billionth of a second in its first firing. When the twenty-foot-wide beam laser was completed in 1978, it was the world's most powerful laser. The shortcoming was the massive amount of energy required to fuse the atoms to create a new source of energy, which was not practical.

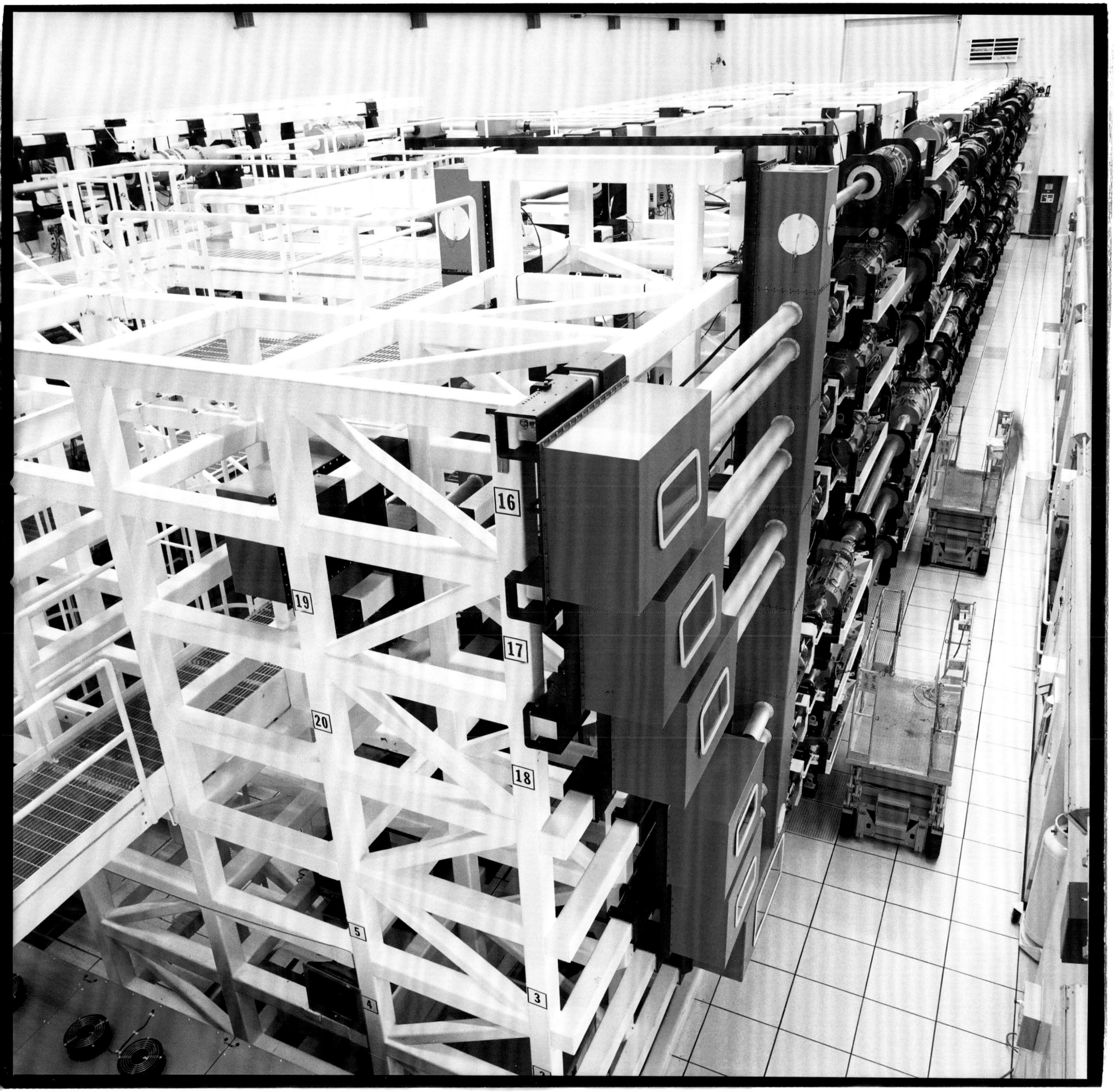
16
19
17
20
18
5
4
3

STANFORD LINEAR ACCELERATOR CENTER TARGET

SLAC, Palo Alto, California
1987

The Linac Coherent Light Source (LCLS) is a free electron laser facility located at SLAC. This two-mile-long particle accelerator is the lab's backbone. This straight accelerator runs underground. Once the scene of major discoveries in particle physics, today the accelerator generates the world's brightest X-rays for SLAC's revolutionary X-ray laser, the Linac Coherent Light Source. Thousands of scientists come to SLAC each year to use LCLS and the Stanford Synchrotron Radiation Lightsource to probe matter in atomic detail. These X-ray studies help scientists understand the fundamental workings of nature and find solutions to real-world problems. The research has contributed to the development of medications for melanoma, the flu, and HIV, and is aiding the fight against Ebola, high blood pressure, and other illnesses. Meanwhile, scientists use X-ray beams for experiments to improve materials for computer chips, jet planes, refinery operations, and "smart windows" that automatically adjust the amount of light coming in. SLAC studies of exotic materials with quirky traits could have a profound impact on society.

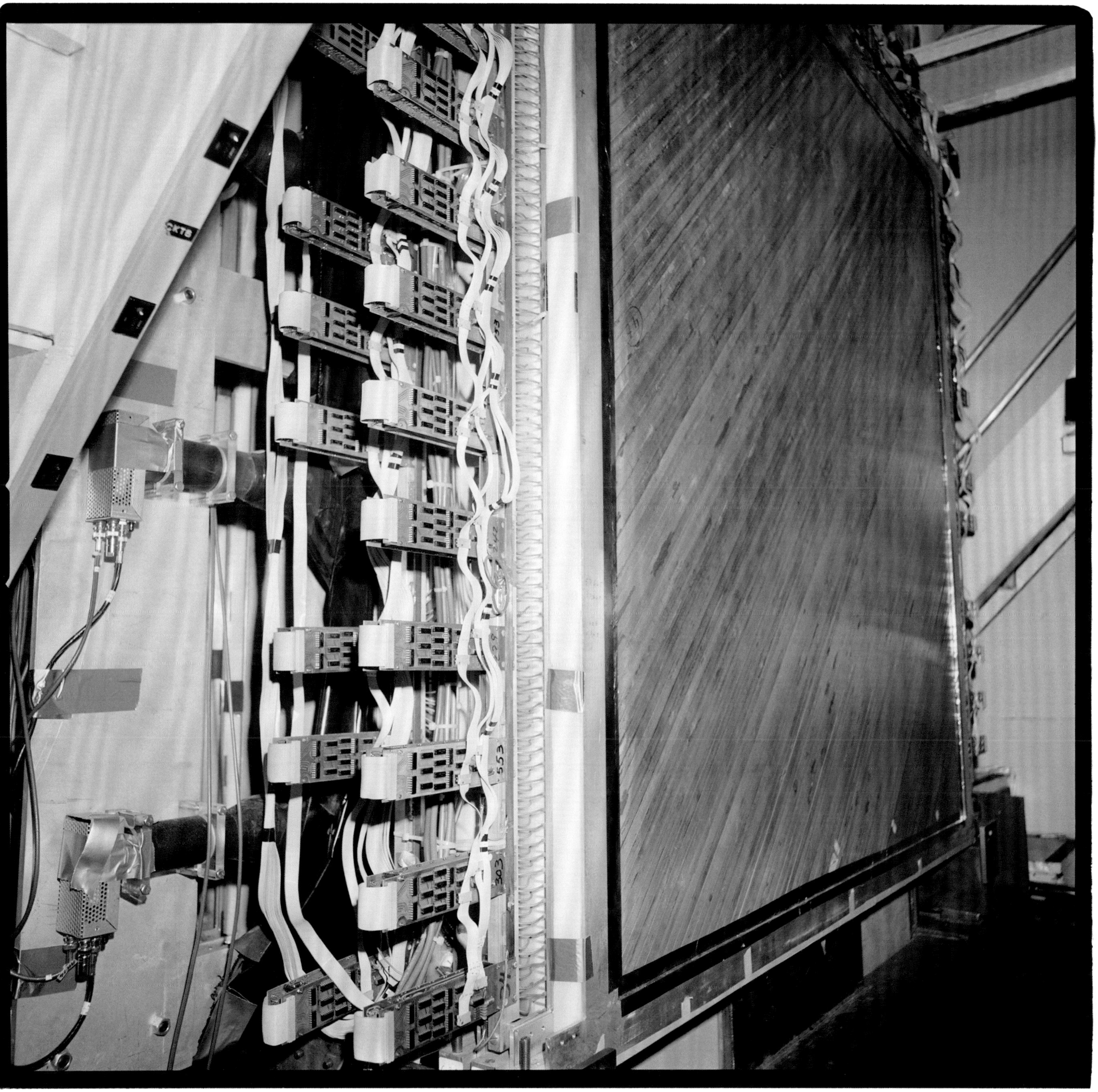

BERKELEY BEVATRON

UC Berkeley, California
1986

The Bevatron was a particle accelerator, a weak-focusing proton synchrotron at Lawrence Berkeley National Laboratory, which began operating in 1954. It was built by the Atomic Energy Commission for US$9 million. *Popular Science* called it a "10,000-Ton Cracker for Invisible Nuts." The antiproton was discovered there in 1955, resulting in the 1959 Nobel Prize in Physics for Emilio Segrè and Owen Chamberlain. The 135-foot-diameter Bevatron was the largest in a series of circular particle accelerators invented by E. O. Lawrence, after whom Lawrence Berkeley and Lawrence Livermore National Labs are named. In addition to the use of the cyclotron for physics, Lawrence also supported its use in research into medical uses of radioisotopes. The Bevatron accelerated protons into a fixed target (the subject of my photograph), and was named for its ability to impart energies of billions of eV. Following World War II, positive and negative muons and pions were observed in cosmic-ray interactions seen in cloud chambers and stacks of nuclear photographic emulsions. The Bevatron was built to be energetic enough to create antiprotons, discovered in 1951, and thus tested the hypothesis that every particle has a corresponding antiparticle. The facility sat proudly atop the Berkeley Hills campus until it was demolished in 2011.

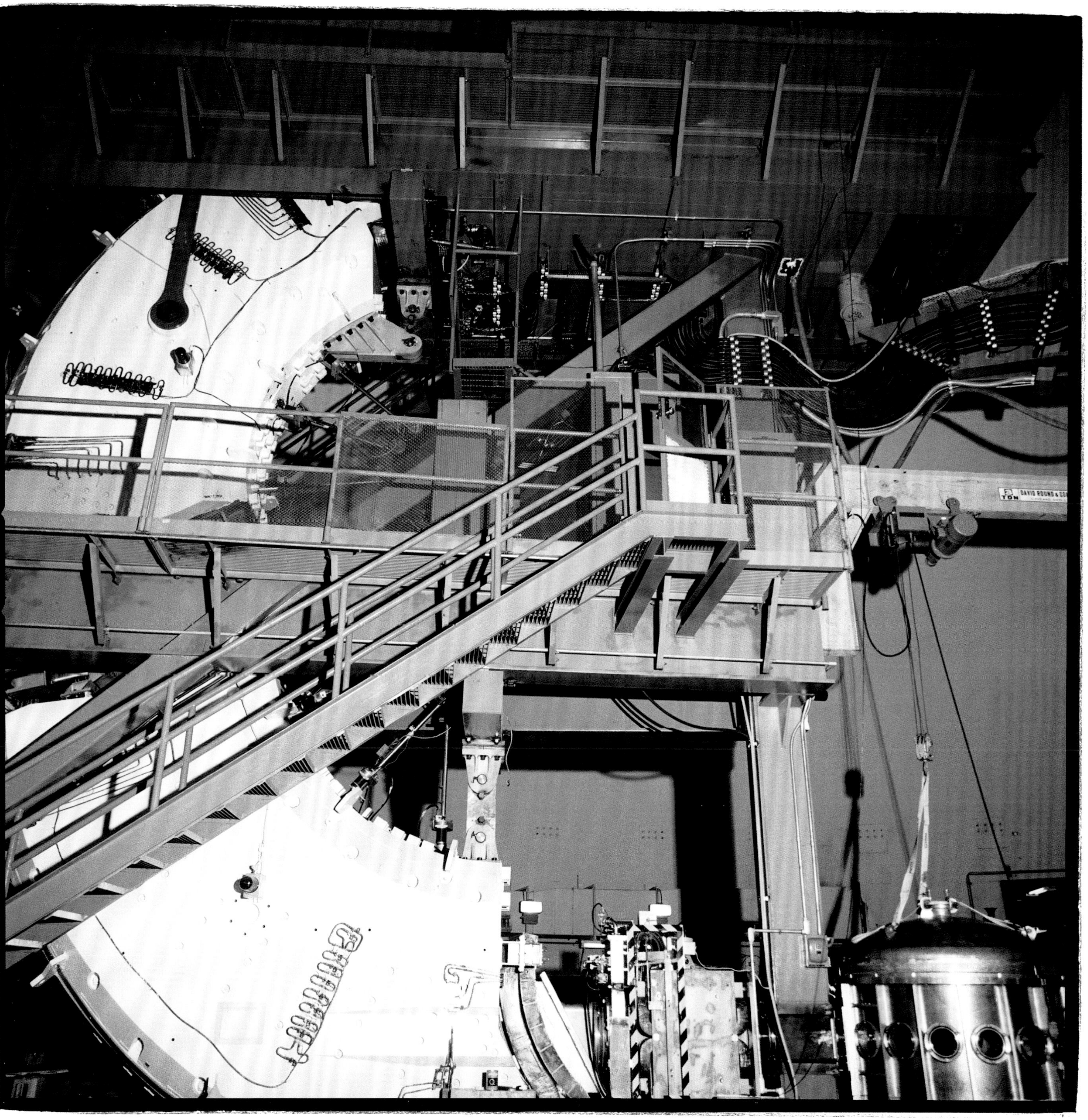
TDM
DAVID ROUND &

LOS ALAMOS LASER BREEDER

Los Alamos, New Mexico
1989

The Trident Laser is a high-power, sub-petawatt class, solid-state laser facility located at Los Alamos National Laboratory in Los Alamos, NM. The Trident Laser consists of three main laser chains (A, B, and C) of neodymium glass amplifiers (or Nd:glass): two are identical longpulse beamslines, A&B, and a third beamline, C, can be operated either in longpulse or in chirped pulse amplification (CPA) shortpulse mode. Los Alamos was selected as the top-secret location for bomb design in late 1942, due to its remoteness, and officially commissioned the next year, under the management of the University of California. At the time it was known as Project Y and was the center for weapons design and overall coordination. It prided itself as the laboratory having the highest number of PhDs per square mile. Other labs, today known as Oak Ridge National Laboratory and the Hanford Site (now decommissioned), concentrated on the production of uranium and plutonium for bomb fuels. Los Alamos was the heart of the project, collecting some of the world's most famous scientists, among them numerous Nobel Prize winners, most notably J. R. Oppenheimer, the "father of the atomic bomb," of the Manhattan Project. The lab's existence was announced to the world in the post-WWII era when it became known universally as Los Alamos. The laser is currently being used for Fast Ignition ICF research, warm dense matter experiments, materials dynamics studies, and laser-matter interaction. When it is activated for a nano-second it consumes more energy than the entire state of New Mexico.

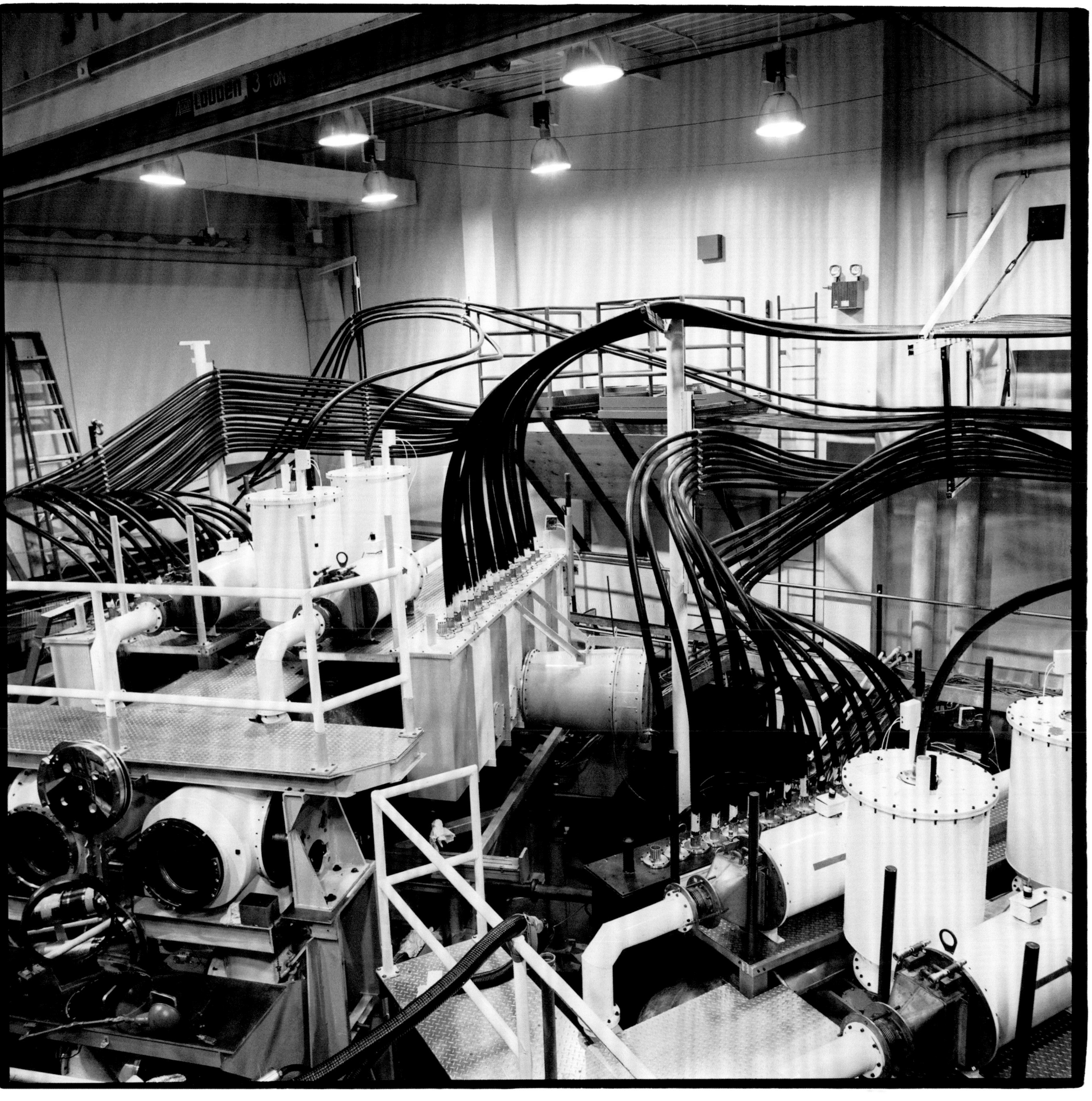
LOUDEN 3 TON

MAGNETIC FUSION

Lawrence Livermore Laboratory,
California
1986

Lawrence Livermore National Laboratory was established in 1952, at the height of the Cold War, to meet urgent national security needs by advancing nuclear weapons science and technology. Fusion, as generated by the sun, is safe, non-polluting, and almost boundless, an ideal source of energy. The basic concept behind fusion is simple: squeeze hydrogen atoms hard enough and they fuse together into helium. Hydrogen is so abundant that unlike fossil fuels or fissionable material like uranium, it will never run out. Scientists have yet to unlock the secrets of keeping a fusion reaction going long enough to generate usable energy. Hence the standing joke: "fusion is 30 years in the future...and always will be." Current study here is investigating the interface between the hot fusion plasma, and the material walls surrounding it for energy production. From its inception, Livermore focused on new weapon design concepts. Physics focused areas include condensed matter and high-pressure physics, optical science and high energy density physics, medical physics and biophysics, and nuclear, particle, and accelerator physics.

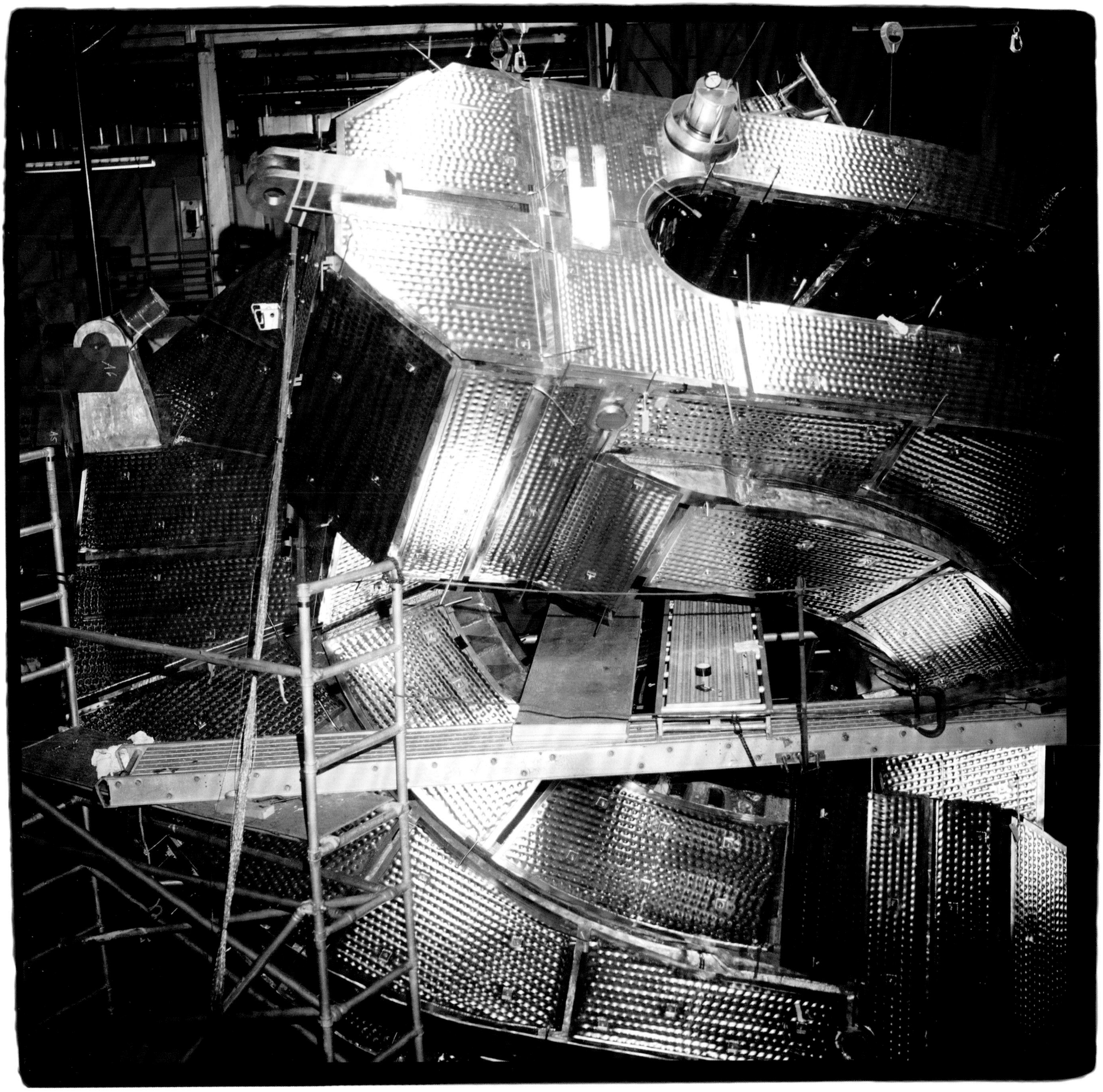

RADIOACTIVE ROBOT

Sandia Laboratories, Albuquerque,
New Mexico
1987

Sandia National Laboratories is a multiprogram laboratory operated and managed by Sandia Corporation, a wholly owned subsidiary of Lockheed Martin Corporation, for the US Department of Energy's National Nuclear Security Administration. Sandia's primary mission is ensuring the US nuclear arsenal is safe, secure, and reliable, and can fully support our nation's deterrence policy, by weaponizing the nuclear explosive package. Sandia is recognized globally as an early robotics pioneer. The Sandia Interior Robot, or SIR (seen here), made a lasting impression on the nation when it was introduced in 1985 as the first truly autonomous interior robot. SIR could perform such dangerous work as disposing of radioactive waste or gathering military intelligence in a hostile environment. It emerged from a program started ten years earlier to develop technologies for detecting interior intrusions for the Department of Energy's nuclear safeguards efforts. In this photograph, a robotic arm is removing a radioactive material from the testing facility surrounded by massive concrete walls to shield the radioactive waves from its employees.

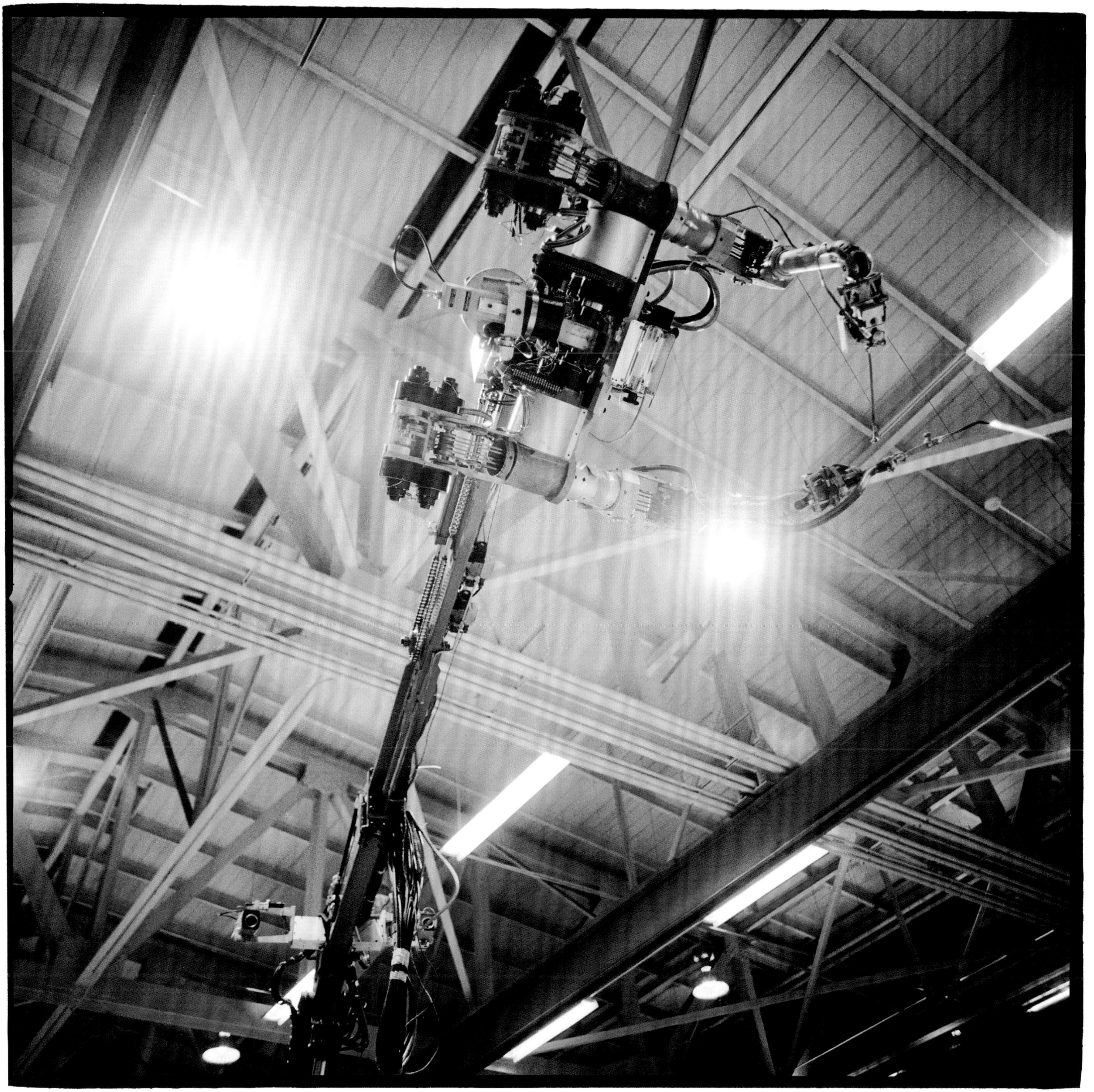

TRON

Lawrence Livermore Laboratory,
California
1986

This image was named for the 1982 movie that was shot at Lawrence Livermore Laboratory, where a boy entered a computer and was lost within its networks. The 10 kJ Shiva laser irradiation facility at LLNL is a major laser experimental facility devoted to inertial confinement fusion (ICF) research. The evolution of Shiva into a reliable experimental facility required the development of engineering technology based on solid-state laser concepts introduced in the 1960s. Shiva has operated continuously, providing up to 28 terawatts (TW) of 1.064 μm optical power to targets. Lawrence Livermore Laboratory experimental laser programs were consolidated into a single division, known as Y Division, in 1972. Since then, increasingly complex and energetic laser systems, each with five to ten times more energy than its predecessor, have enabled cutting-edge research in ICF, high energy density science, nuclear weapons stockpile stewardship, discovery science, and laser fusion energy. This is a small portion of the massive Shiva laser facility, which is longer than a football field.

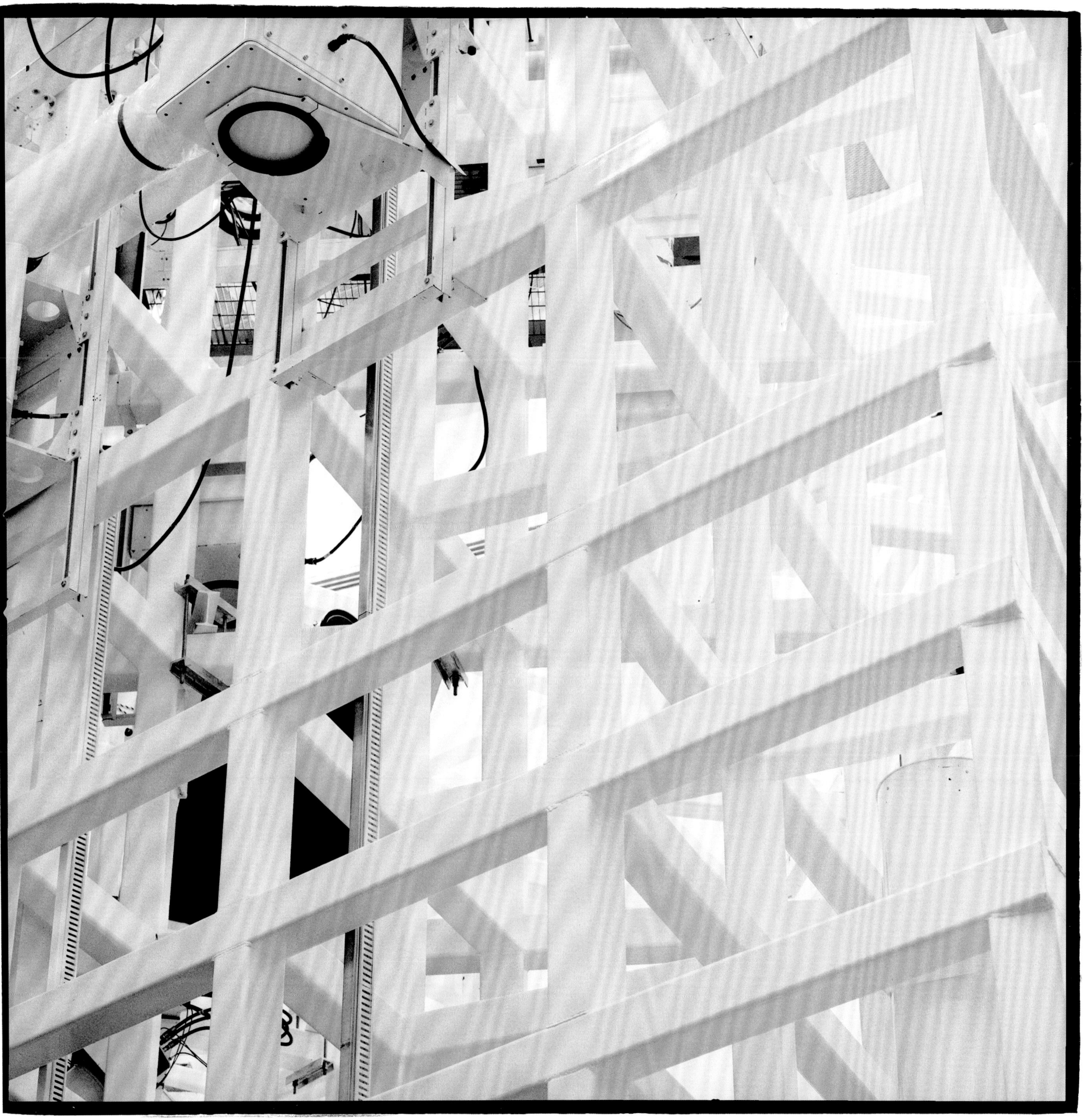

DAMS

CONCRETE ICON

Grand Coulee Dam,
Washington
1978

Grand Coulee Dam provides water to irrigate 600,000 acres in the Columbia Basin Project. It is a primary factor in controlling floods on the Columbia River. The proposal to build the dam was the focus of a bitter debate during the 1920s. One group wanted to irrigate the ancient Grand Coulee with a gravity canal, while the other pursued a high dam and pumping scheme. The gravity dam supporters won. The dam took eight years to build, employed thousands during the Great Depression, and, when completed in 1942, provided the enormous electrical power necessary to make aluminum, essential for World War II production of planes and ships. The Grand Coulee Dam project, a massive irrigation and hydroelectric project, gained full momentum by the mid-1960s. Marcel Breuer and Associates, hired by the US Bureau of Reclamation, designed the third power plant. The resulting structure is a significant design statement of the era, displaying both the solid strength of reinforced concrete and the expressive forms that it can produce in a Brutalist style. It is a tour de force of design, strength, and form, an altar to concrete. A print of this image was purchased by the Breuer office in New York.

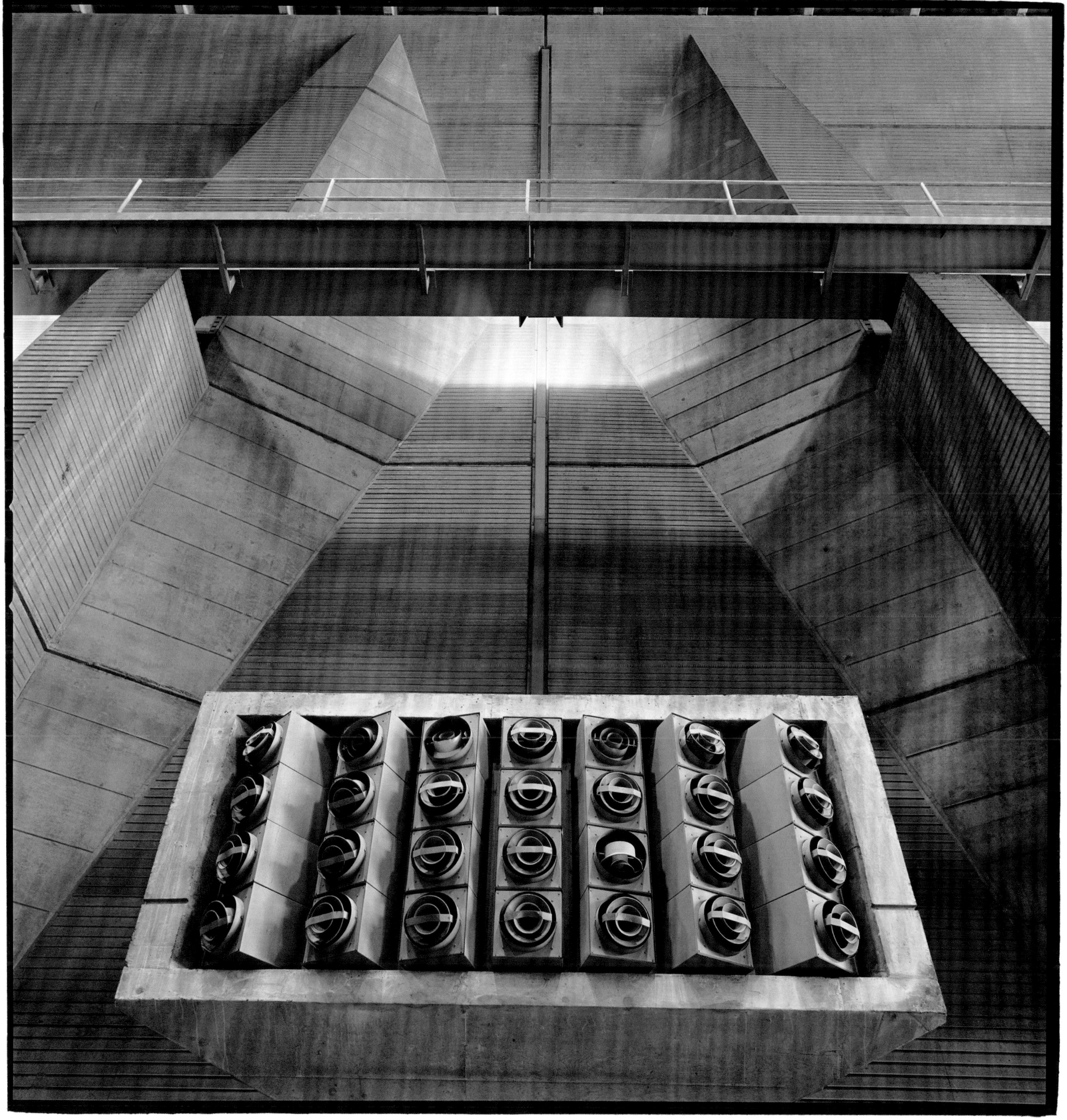

HOOVER DAM OVERHEAD

Boulder City, Nevada
1975

Hoover Dam is an arch-gravity dam that resists the pressure of water by its weight, using the force of gravity and the arch design. Hoover Dam curves upstream in a narrowing passage that directs the water pressure against the canyon rock walls, providing the force to compress and strengthen the dam. It was the first structure built to contain more masonry than the historical record-holder, the Great Pyramid at Giza. The dam is perched in the Black Canyon of the Colorado River. It was constructed between 1931 and 1936, and was dedicated by President Franklin D. Roosevelt. The winning bid to build the dam was submitted by a consortium called Six Companies, Inc., which employed 5,000 workers during construction. It would cost US$860 million in today's dollars. After the dam was completed and the lake began to fill, large numbers of significant leaks were found. New holes were drilled from inspection galleries inside the dam into the surrounding bedrock—it took nine years to rectify. Water from Lake Mead serves 18 million people in Arizona, Nevada, and California and supplies the irrigation of over 1,000,000 acres. Known as Boulder Dam in 1933, it was officially renamed Hoover Dam for President Herbert Hoover by a joint resolution of Congress in 1947.

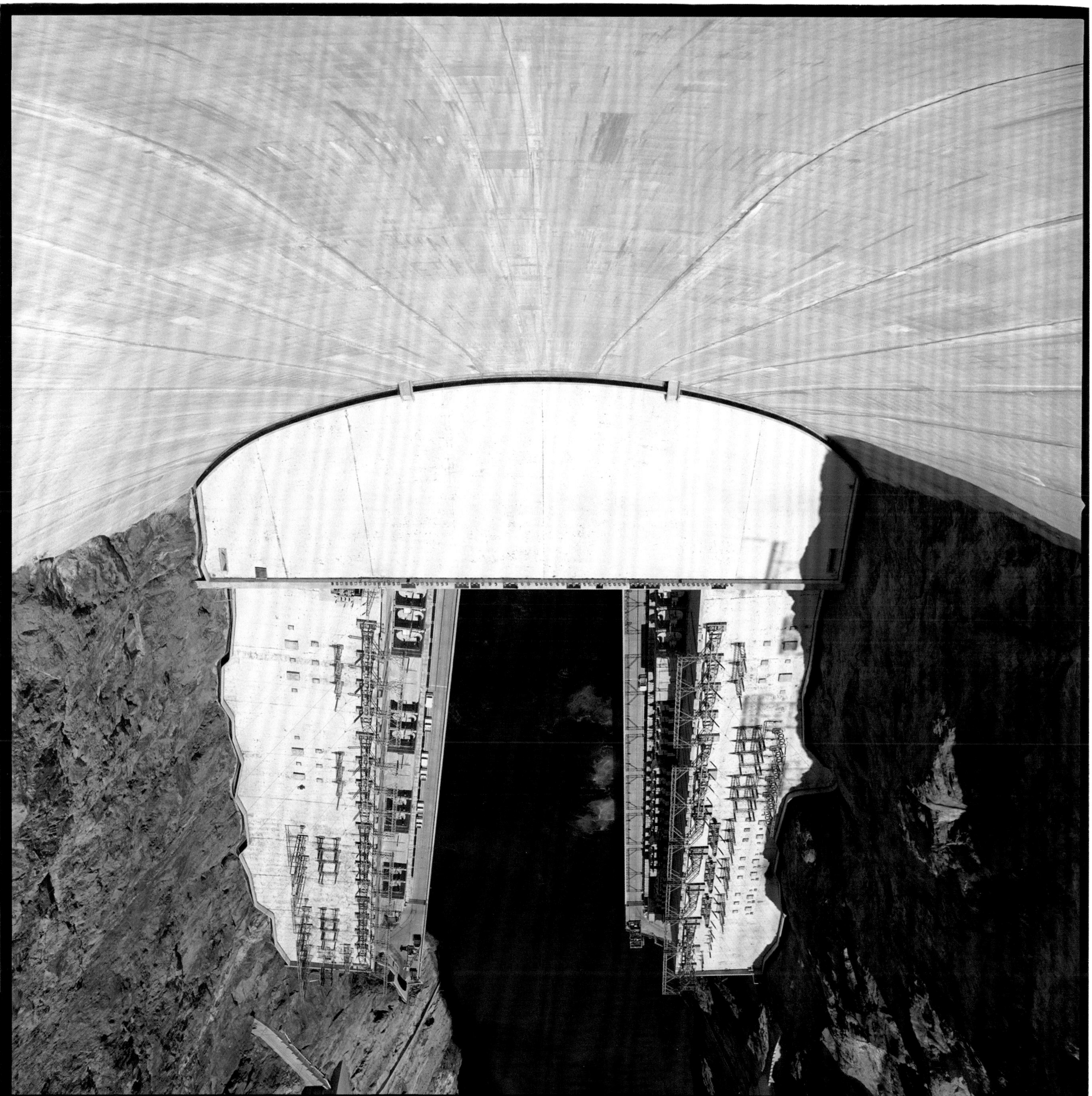

DIVERSION PIPES

Shasta Dam, Shasta, California
1980

Shasta Dam, which serves mainly to provide flood control and carryover water storage for the dry season, contributes significantly to irrigation in the Sacramento Valley. Even before its dedication, Shasta Dam served an important role in World War II. During the war years, many of the people who worked at the dam were women and high school students on "non-hazardous jobs." The dam played another part in World War II, even before completion, supplying much-needed electricity to shipyards and aircraft factories in central California. The Shasta Dam still plays a vital part in the management of state water resources, supplying substantial water to the Bay Area. A gravity structure, the dam stands 602 feet above the foundations. It is 3,460 feet long, with a maximum thickness of 543 feet. Shasta Dam was considered one of the greatest engineering feats in the world upon its completion in 1945. The dam forms a reservoir called Shasta Lake, which is the largest human-made lake in California.

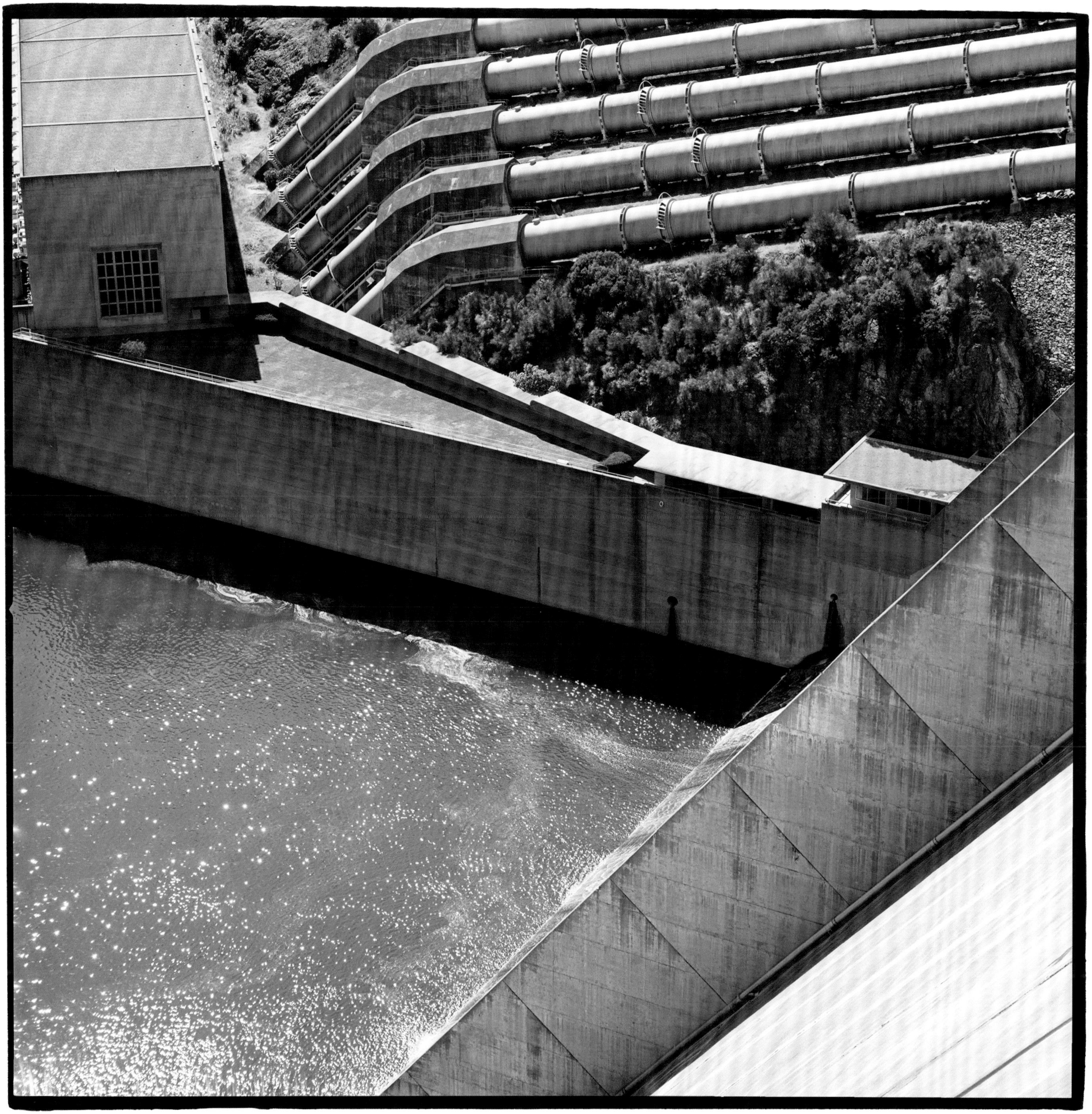

ROSS DAM

Skagit River, Washington
1990

Ross Dam, originally called Ruby Dam, is a concrete thin arch dam across the Skagit River, forming Ross Lake. Ross Dam was constructed primarily to generate hydroelectricity from the massive elevation drop of over 1,000 feet from the Canada-US border to Nehalem, WA. It was built in three stages between 1937 and 1949, and currently stands 540 feet high. Ross Dam can generate up to 460 MW of electricity; hydro-electric dams provide approximately 92% of the electricity used in Seattle. One kilowatt provides annual electricity to one thousand homes. In 1943, a consortium of contractors including Morrison-Knudsen began new construction on the dam. Energy demands during World War II coincided with an energy shortage in Seattle, requiring that the dam be constructed quickly; nonetheless, Ross Dam did not generate any power until many years after the war ended. A fourth stage of construction was planned for the dam; however, in 1984, Seattle City Light made an electricity-purchasing agreement with British Columbia that delayed any further expansion of the dam for 80 years. The concrete waffling, shown in this photograph, was intended to increase the 700-foot elevation above the river height, but when Seattle City Light decided not to proceed with construction, this stepped concrete left remarkable patterns in the Ross Dam face.

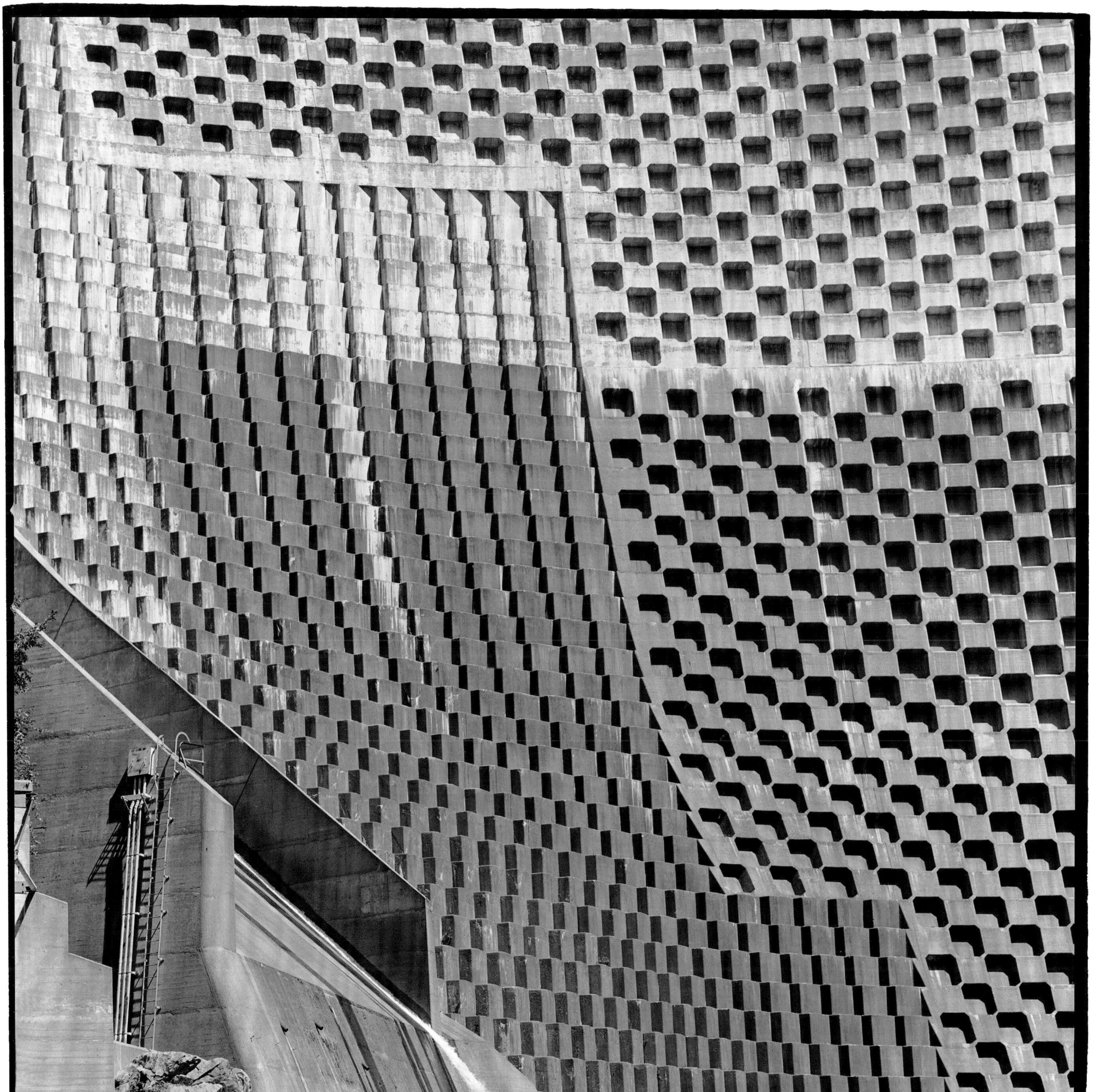

HOOVER SECTIONAL

Boulder City, Nevada
1975

Hoover Dam impounds Lake Mead, the largest reservoir in the United States, now at its lowest level in history. As the technology of electric power transmission improved, the Lower Colorado was considered for its hydroelectric-power potential. A massive concrete arch-gravity dam, the curving arch of the Hoover Dam transmits the water's force into the abutments, in this case the rock walls of the canyon. Following the completion of the dam, the entrances to the two outer diversion tunnels were sealed with large concrete plugs. In 1902, the Edison Electric Company of Los Angeles surveyed the river in the hope of building a 40-foot (12 m) rock dam that could generate 10,000 horsepower (7,500 kW). Hoover Dam now generates 4 billion kWh, supplying energy to 1.3 million homes. The downstream halves of the tunnels following the inner plugs are now the main bodies of the spillway tunnels. The initial plans for the facade of the dam, the power plant, the outlet tunnels, and ornaments clashed with the modern look of an arch dam. The Bureau of Reclamation, more concerned with functionality, adorned it with a Deco-Gothic-inspired balustrade, eagle statues, and a monument. Surrounding the base of the monument is a terrazzo floor embedded with a "star map." The map depicts the Northern Hemisphere sky at the moment of President Roosevelt's dedication of the Hoover Dam. This is intended to help future astronomers calculate the exact date of dedication.

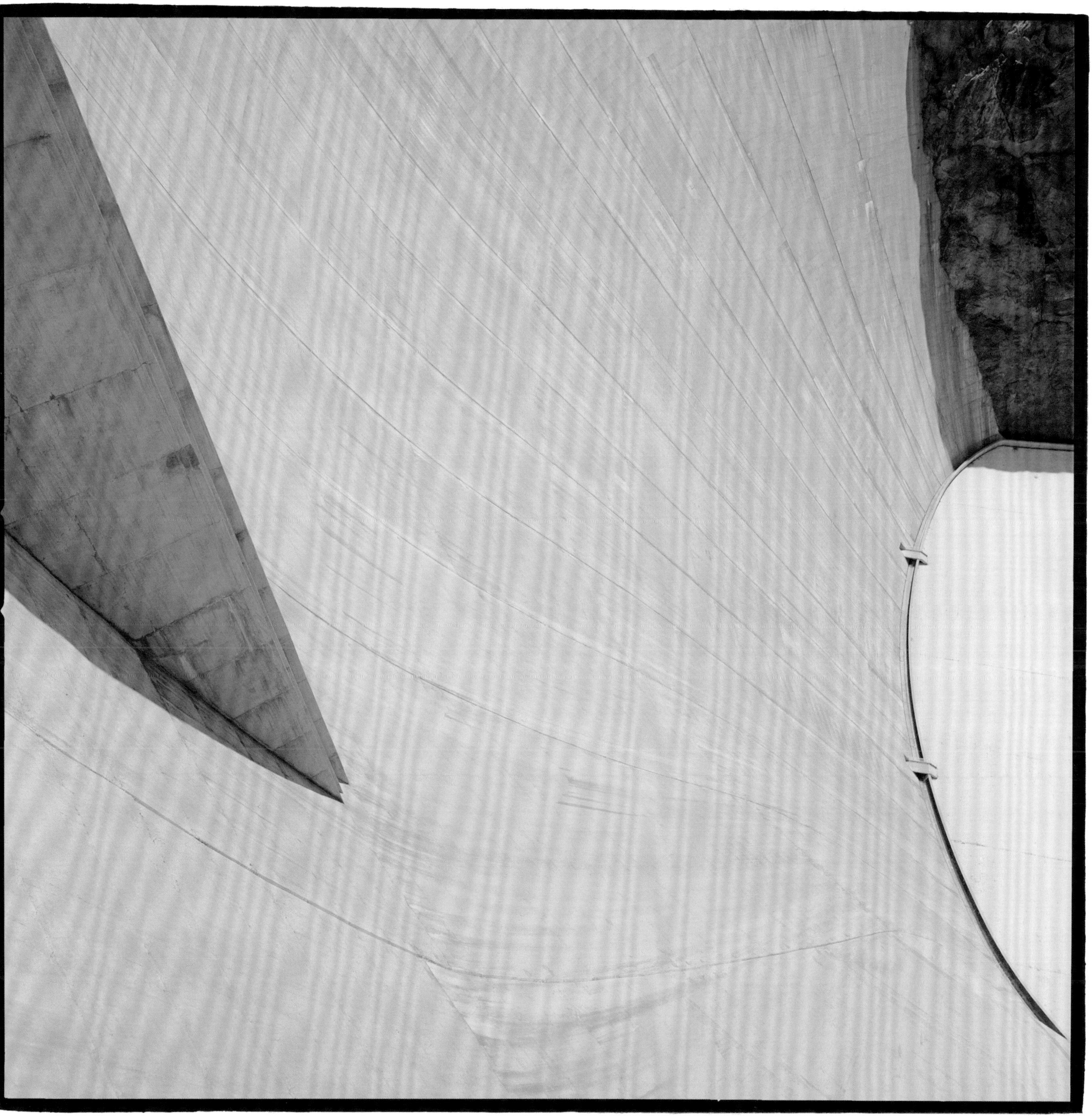

ASWAN DAM

Aswan, Egypt
1985

The Aswan High Dam is the world's largest dam, built across the Nile at Aswan, Egypt, between 1960 and 1970. In 1952, the Greek-Egyptian engineer Adrian Daninos began to develop the plan of the new Aswan Dam. The Aswan High Dam is 13,000 feet long and 364 feet tall. The enormous rock and clay dam was designed by the Soviet Hydroproject Institute. 25,000 Egyptian engineers and workers contributed to the construction. Aswan Dam has brought protection from floods and droughts, an increase in agricultural productivity and employment, electricity production, and improved navigation that benefits tourism. Conversely, the dam flooded a large area, and over 100,000 people were displaced. Numerous archaeological sites were submerged, but some were relocated, including the famous Abu Simbel Temples. The giant reservoir created by the dam was named in President Nasser's honor. The Aswan Dam brought the Nile's devastating floods to an end, reclaimed 100,000 acres of desert land for cultivation, and made additional crops possible on 800,000 other acres. The dam's 12 giant Soviet-built turbines produce as much as 10 billion kWh annually, providing a tremendous boost to the Egyptian economy and electricity into many villages. The water stored in Lake Nasser is shared by Egypt and Sudan, and was crucial during the African drought years of 1984 to 1988.

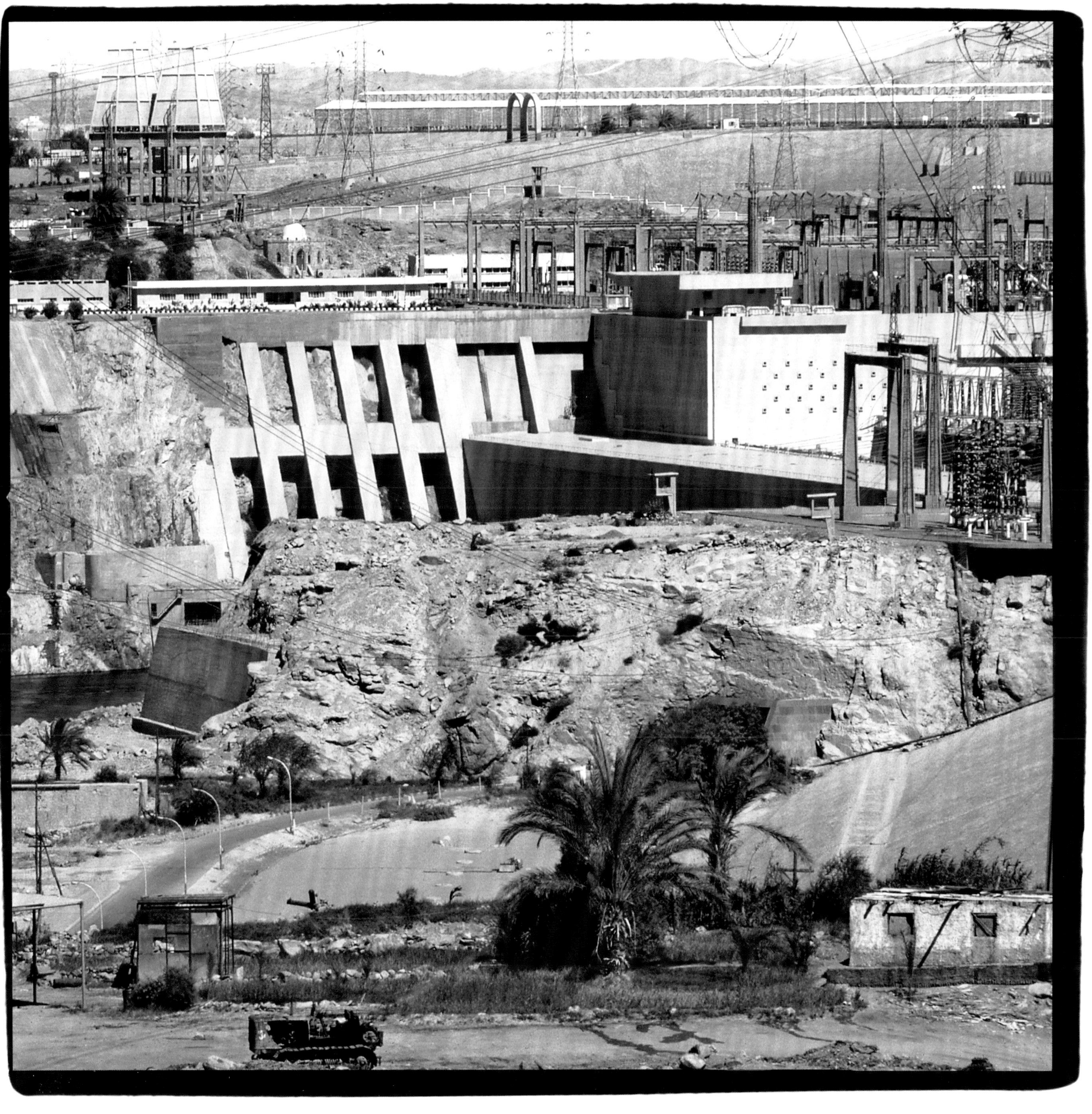

CONSTRUCTION

Grand Coulee Dam, Grand Coulee, Washington
1978

Grand Coulee Dam is a concrete gravity dam on the Columbia River in Washington, built to produce hydroelectric power and provide irrigation water. Constructed between 1933 and 1942, power from the Grand Coulee Dam fueled the growing industries of the Northwest United States during World War II. President Roosevelt envisioned the dam as part of his New Deal under the Public Works Administration; it would create jobs, farming opportunities, and would pay for itself. The reservoir is called Franklin Delano Roosevelt Lake, named after the president. Everything about Grand Coulee Dam is large—it is one of the largest structures ever built by humankind—a mass of concrete standing 550 feet high and 5,223 feet long, just shy of a mile. Grand Coulee Dam contains 12 million cubic yards of concrete, enough to build a highway from Seattle to Miami. More massive than the Great Pyramid of Giza, Grand Coulee Dam is listed by the American Society of Civil Engineers as one of the seven civil engineering wonders of the United States.

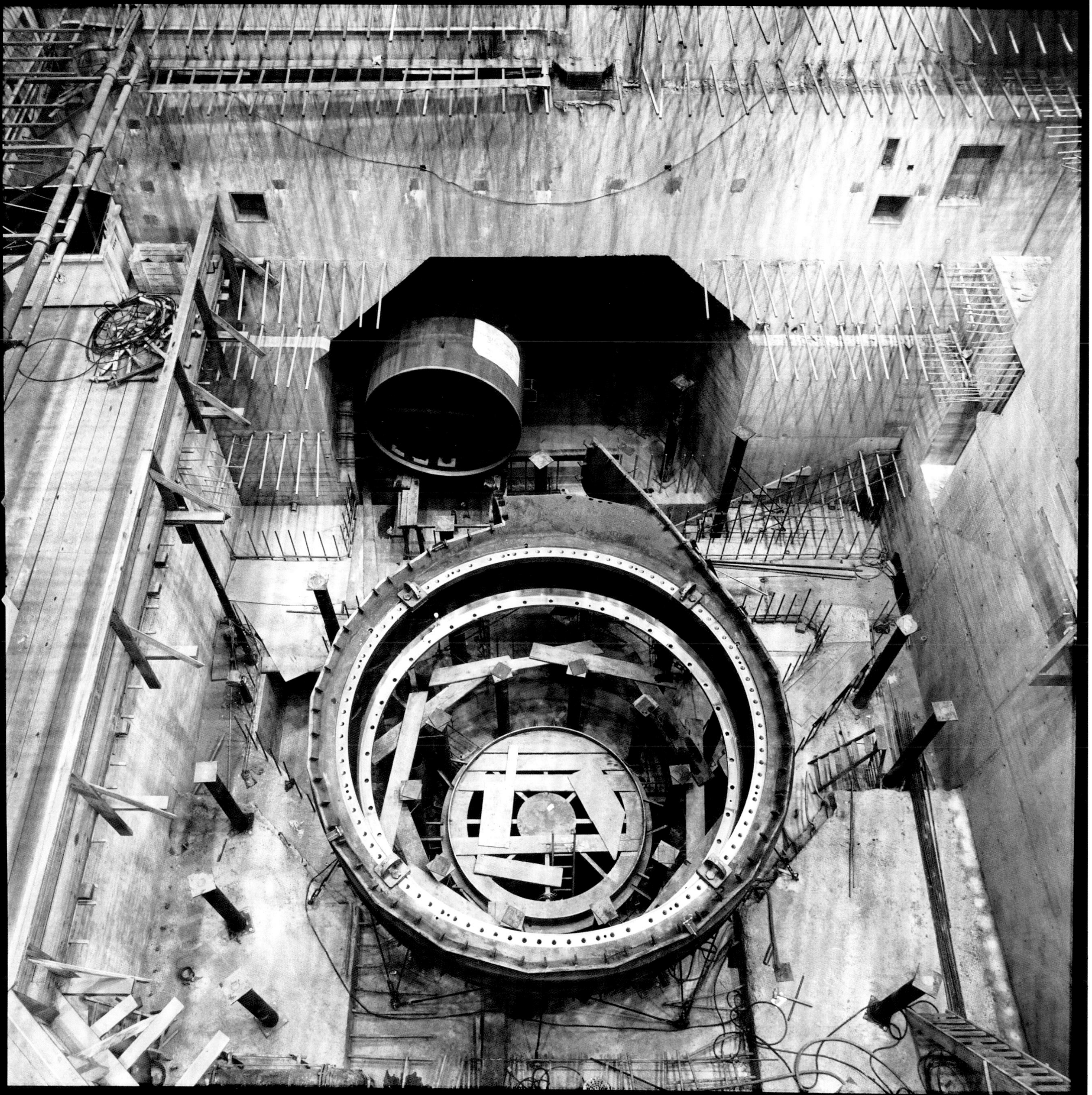

THREE GORGES DAM

Yichang, Hubei province,
China
2015

The Three Gorges Dam is the world's largest hydropower generation project. A straight-crested concrete gravity structure, the Three Gorges Dam is 2,335 meters (7,660 feet) long with a maximum height of 185 meters (607 feet). It incorporates 28 million cubic meters (37 million cubic yards) of concrete and 463,000 metric tons of steel into its design. The dam has created an immense deepwater reservoir allowing oceangoing freighters to navigate 2,250 km (1,400 miles) inland from Shanghai on the East China Sea to the inland city of Chongqing. It spans the Yangtze River by the town of Sandouping, in Yiling District. The Three Gorges Dam has been the world's largest power station in terms of installed capacity (22,500 MW) since 2012. In 2018, the dam generated 101.6 terawatt-hours (TWh), breaking its previous record, but was still slightly lower than the Itaipú Dam, which straddles the Brazil and Paraguay border, and which had set the world record in 2016 after producing 103.1 terawatt-hours. The dam body was completed in 2006. The power plant of the dam project was completed and fully functional as of July 4, 2012. The design incorporates state-of-the-art large turbines. There is also an inventive ship ladder on one side that transports ships from top to bottom outside the river. The annual electricity generation in 2015 was 87 TWh, which is 20 times more than the Hoover Dam.

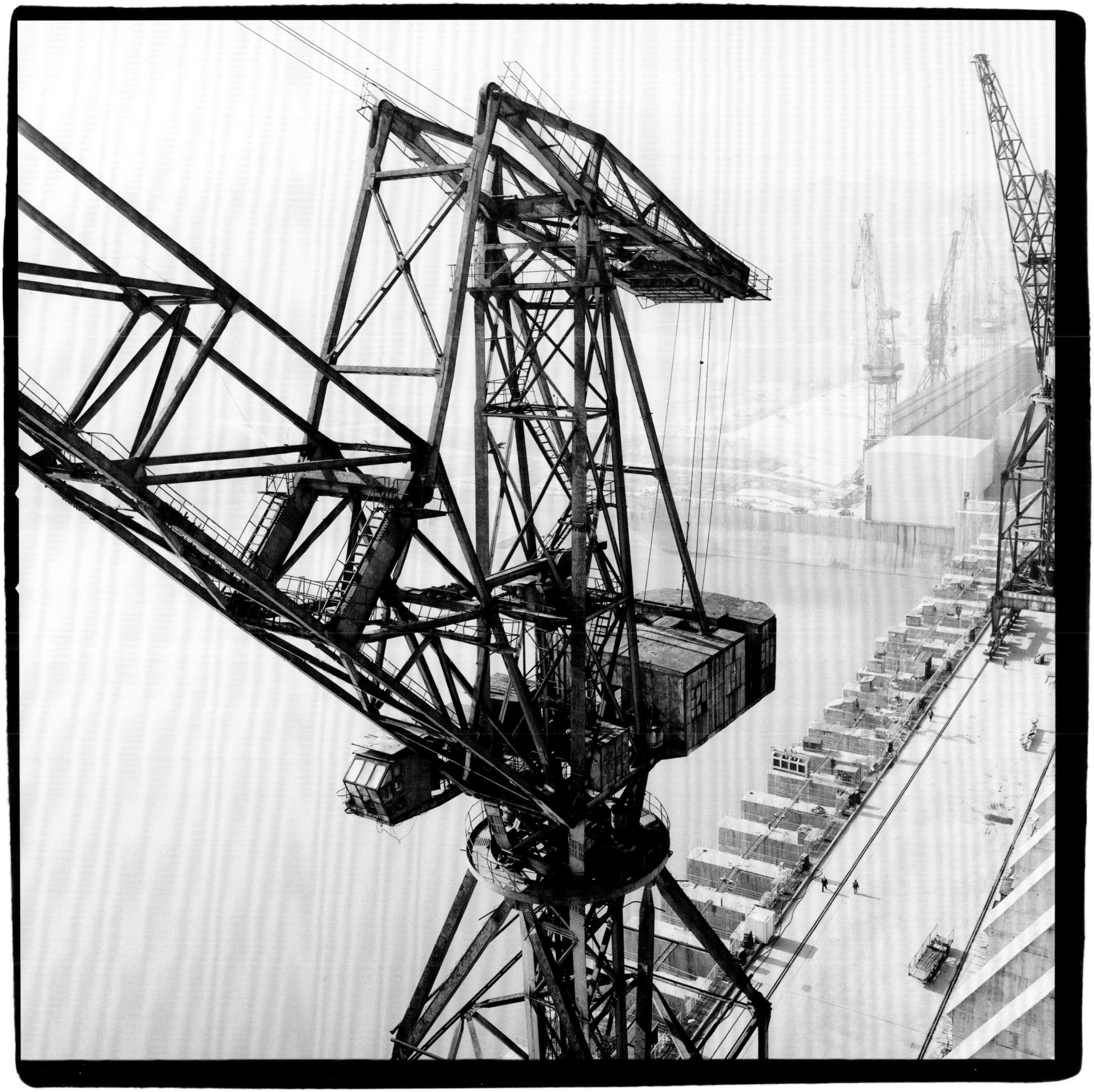

SHASTA DAM SPILLWAY

Lake Shasta, Sacramento River,
California
1981

The Shasta Power Plant is located just below Shasta Dam. Water from the dam is released through five 15-foot penstocks leading to the five main generating units and two station service units. Water released to meet downstream commitments passes through the generators, causing them to spin, generating clean, inexpensive hydroelectric power for distribution to the western US power grid. Power generation at Shasta Dam is very closely tied to water demand: as the reservoir water is called upon to meet water needs downstream, it is sent through generators for power production. The sale of generated power at the Shasta Power Plant is managed by the Department of Energy's Western Area Power Administration, which meets the needs of consumers in the western United States. The sale of this electricity produces US$50 million in revenue annually to the federal government. With a hydraulic head of 330 feet, the dam is capable of generating 676 megawatts (MW) from five turbines—a pair of 125 MW units and three 142 MW units. Two smaller turbines generate power for operations at the dam itself.

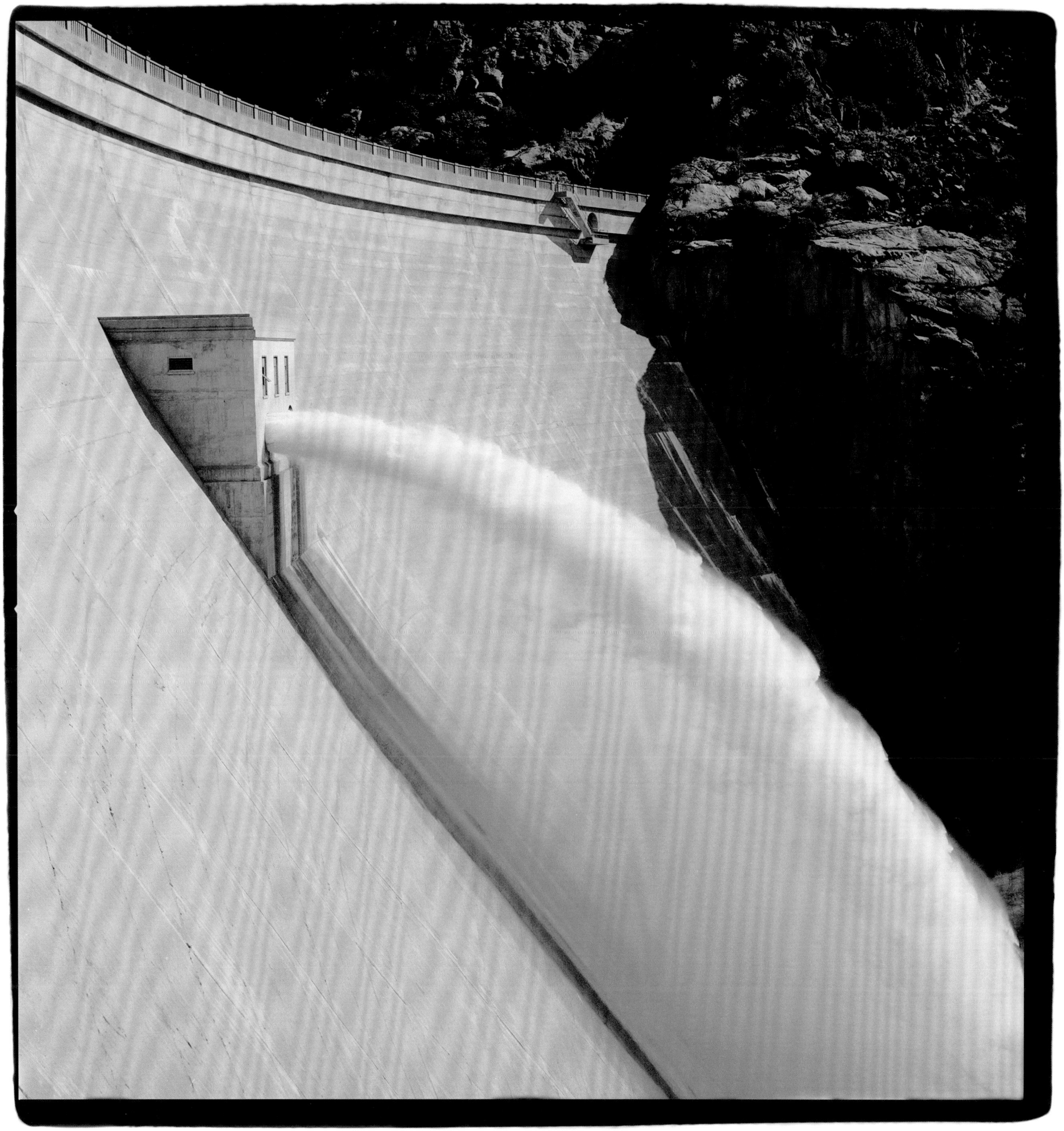

ENERGY

NORTH SEA OIL RIG

Stavanger, Norway
1988

North Sea oil is a mixture of hydrocarbons, comprising liquid petroleum and natural gas, produced from petroleum reservoirs beneath the North Sea. Commercial extraction of oil on the shores of the North Sea dates back to 1851. However, it was not until 1975 that a small entrepreneurial American company, Hamilton Brothers, working in the Argyle field, brought the first British oil ashore, followed by BP in the massive Forties field. The exploration of the North Sea has been a story of continually pushing the edges of the technology of exploitation (in terms of what can be produced); and later the technologies of 2-D seismic discovery and evaluation. When it peaked in 1999, production of North Sea oil was nearly 6 million barrels per day. Offshore oil platforms can cost up to US$600,000 a day to operate. As of January 2015, the North Sea was the world's most active offshore drilling region with 173 active rigs drilling. Norway has 11.2 billion barrels of confirmed oil reserves, the largest of any European country

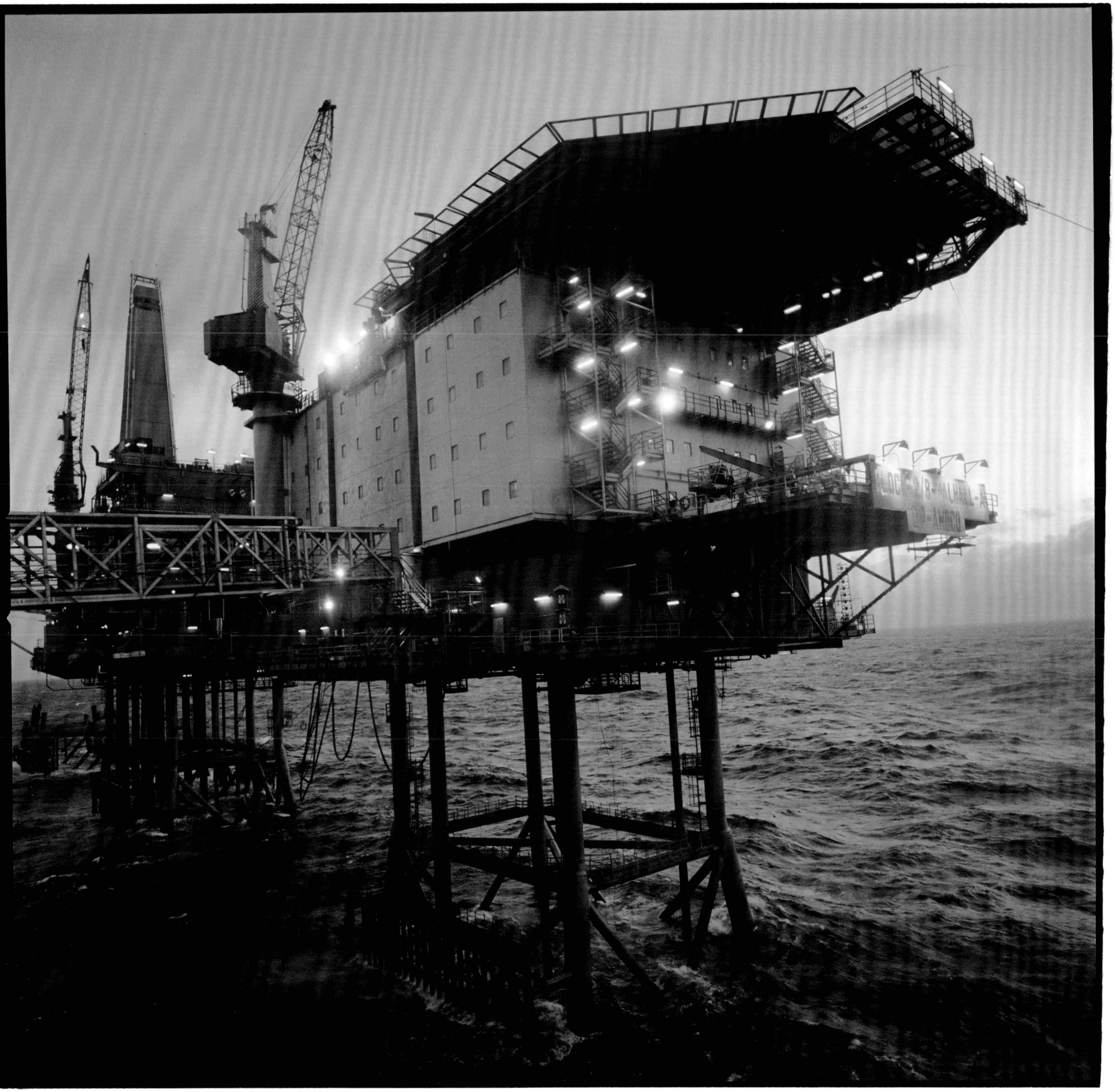

NUCLEAR PLANT COOLANT PIPES

Salem Nuclear Power Plant, Lower Alloways Creek, New Jersey
1995

Nuclear reactors are used at power plants for electricity generation. Heat from nuclear fission is passed to a working fluid (water or gas), which in turn runs through steam turbines. Nuclear reactors convert the energy released by controlled nuclear fission into thermal energy for further conversion to mechanical or electrical forms. When a large fissile atomic nucleus such as uranium-235 or plutonium-239 absorbs a neutron, it may undergo nuclear fission. The heavy nucleus splits into two or more lighter nuclei (the fission products), releasing kinetic energy, gamma radiation, and free neutrons. A portion of these neutrons may be absorbed by other fissile atoms and trigger further fission events, which release more neutrons, and so on. This is known as a nuclear chain reaction. To control such a nuclear chain reaction, control rods containing neutron poisons and neutron moderators can change the portion of neutrons that will go on to cause more fission. Water-cooled reactors constitute the great majority of operational nuclear reactors: 93% of the world's nuclear reactors are water cooled, providing about 95% of the world's total nuclear generation capacity. The Salem Nuclear Power Plant is a two-unit pressurized water reactor nuclear power plant located in Lower Alloways Creek Township, in Salem County, NJ.

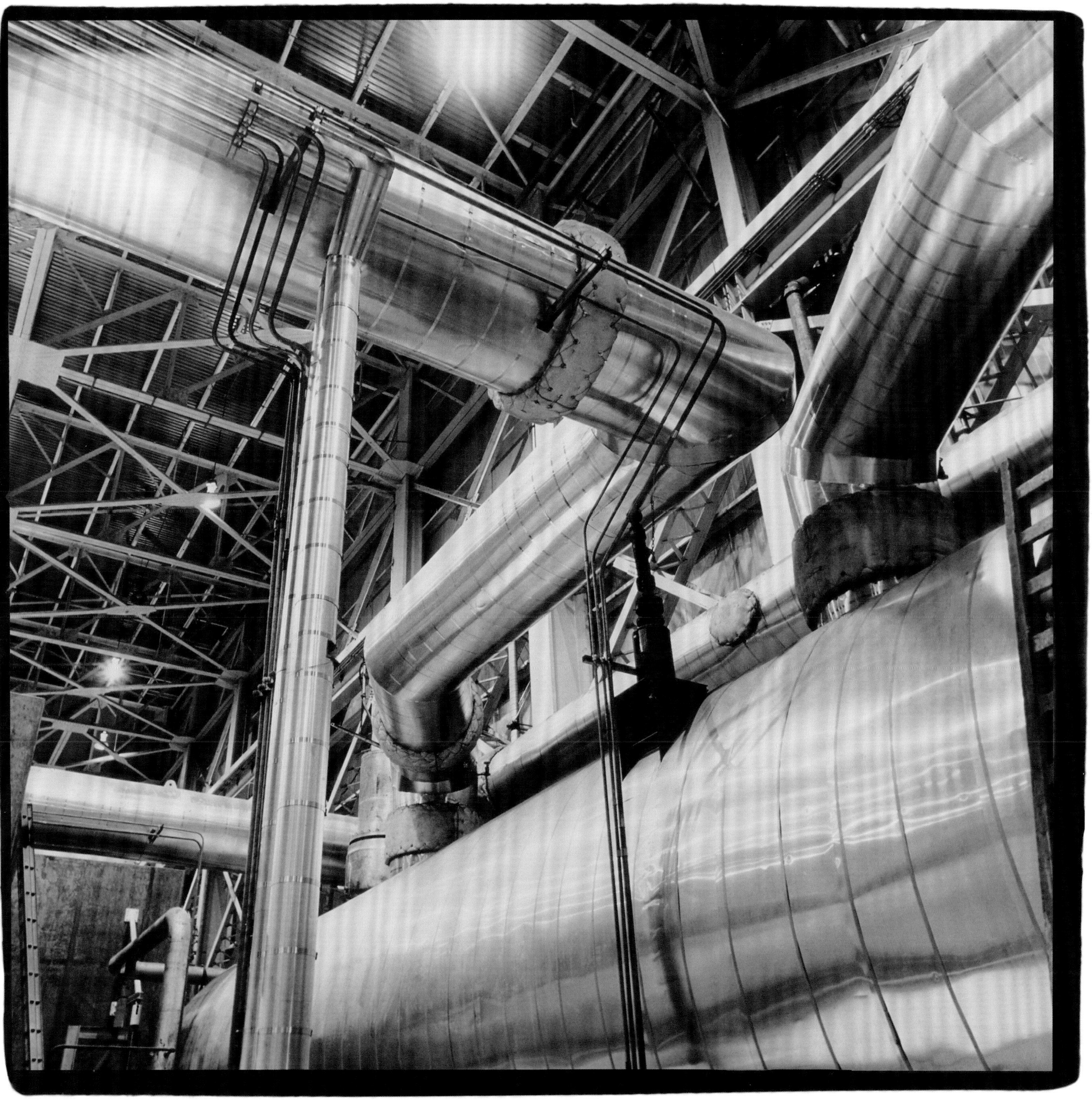

HANFORD COOLING TOWER

Benton County, Washington
1978

The Department of Energy's Hanford Site is a 586-square-mile complex, home to nine former plutonium production reactors and associated processing facilities. Established in 1943 as part of the Manhattan Project, the site was home to the B Reactor, the first full-scale plutonium production reactor in the world. Plutonium manufactured at the site was used in the first nuclear bomb, and in Fat Man, the bomb detonated over Nagasaki, Japan. During the Cold War, the project included nine nuclear reactors and five large plutonium processing complexes. The weapons production reactors were decommissioned at the end of the Cold War and left behind 53 million US gallons (200,000 m3) of waste. Hanford is the most contaminated nuclear site in the United States. Today, workers are involved in an environmental cleanup project of immense proportions. The plutonium production process generated billions of gallons of liquid waste and millions of tons of solid waste. The Vit Plant is a major element of the clean-up effort. It will safely process millions of gallons of radioactive liquid waste that remain in underground tanks indefinitely.

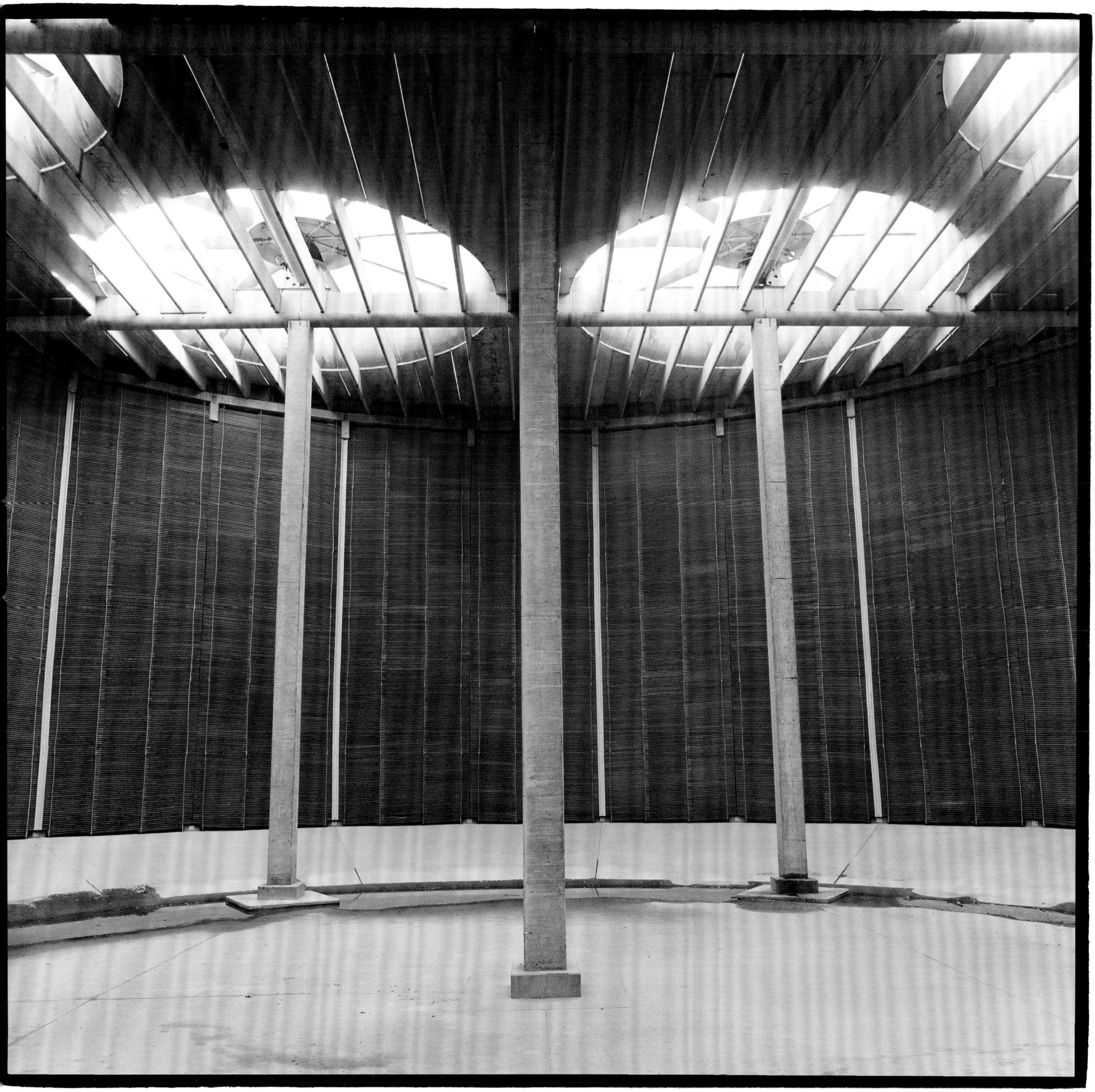

SOLAR ONE

Mojave Desert, Daggatt-Barstow,
California
1985

Solar One was a pilot solar-thermal project built in the Mojave Desert just east of Barstow, CA. It was the first test of a large-scale thermal solar power tower plant. Solar One was completed in 1981, and was operational from 1982 to 1988. This system used hundreds of flat sun-tracking mirrors called heliostats to reflect and concentrate the sun's energy onto a 100-meter-tall central receiving tower, which drove a generating turbine to create electricity through steam-powered turbines. The energy was concentrated as much as 1,500 times the energy coming in from the sun, at about 10 megawatts, which could power 10,000 homes. Solar One generated power until 1988. A redesign of the solar project resulted in Solar Two, completed in 1995. Solar Two was in operation until 1999, and reached its peak producing 10 megawatts of power (enough for 7,500 homes). The central tower of Solar One and Solar Two was torn down in 2009.

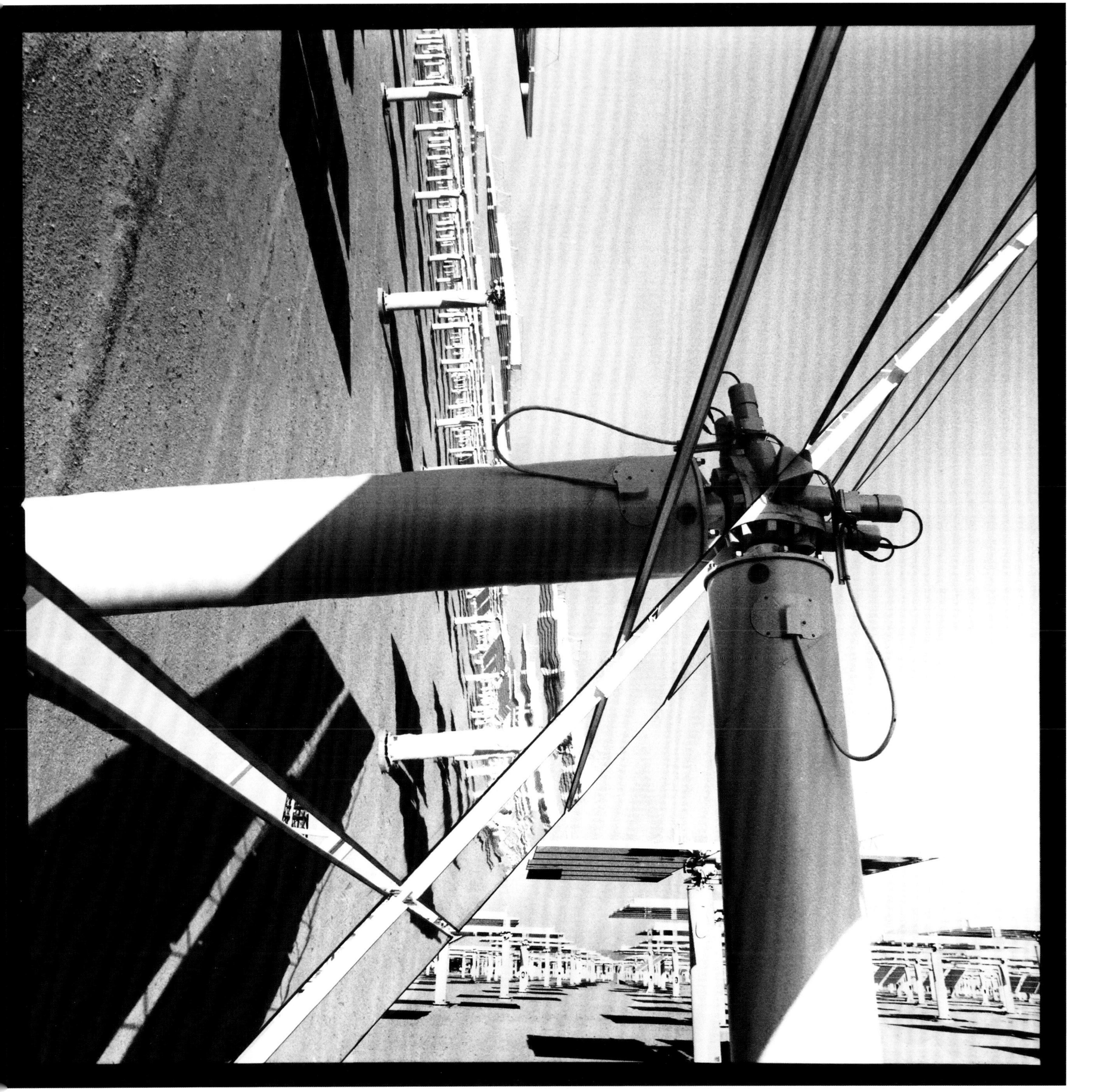

COAL LIQUEFACTION

Baytown, Texas
1981

Coal liquefaction was a process that converted coal into liquid fuels or petrochemicals. There were two processes used to accomplish this: the "indirect route" and the "direct route." The indirect route gasified coal with steam and oxygen to produce a synthesis gas (syngas), which was then cleaned to rid the gas of dust, tar, and acid gases. The second step reacted the synthesis gas with a catalyst in the Fischer-Tropsch process, which converted the syngas into a range of hydrocarbon fuels such as gasoline, diesel, and methanol. In the direct route, coal was pulverized and reacted with a catalyst, then hydrogen was added under high pressures and temperatures in the presence of a solvent to produce a raw liquid fuel. Part of the complexity and problem with production, this raw fuel then required refining in order to yield acceptable transportation fuels, up to 250 tons a day. Coal liquefaction was originally developed at the beginning of the twentieth century. In 1977, design commenced for a plant built by Carter Oil, in Baytown, TX. The plant was closed and dismantled in 1982.

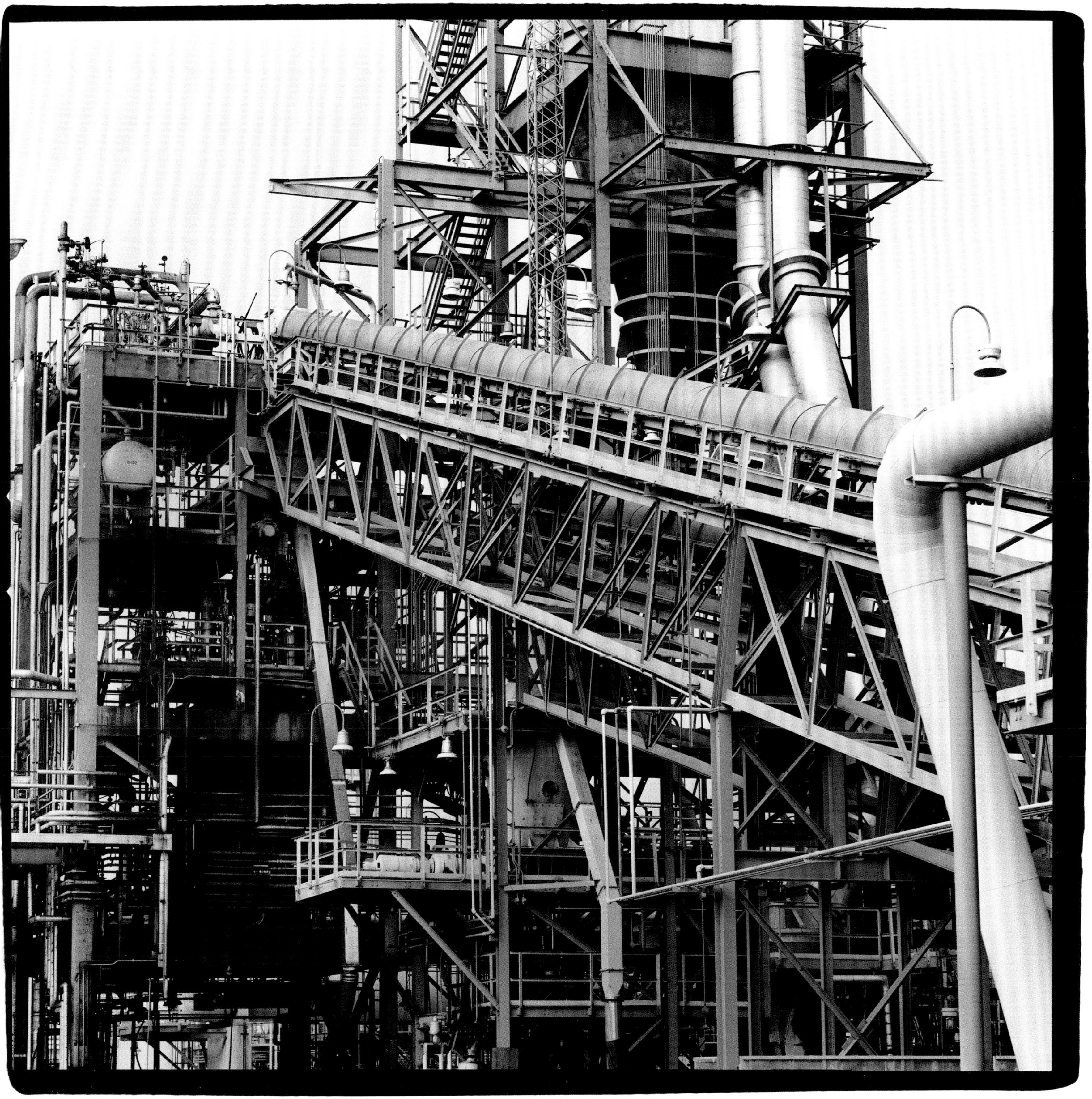

GEOTHERMAL FIELD

Santa Rosa, Sonoma,
California
2016

The Geysers is the world's largest geothermal field spanning 30 square miles in Sonoma, Lake, and Mendocino counties in California. Steam for the power plants is harnessed from a greywacke sandstone reservoir located at the top of a heterogeneous mix of low permeability rocks. Power from the Geysers provides electricity to Sonoma, Mendocino, Marin, and Napa counties. It is estimated that the development meets 60% of the power demand for the coastal region between the Golden Gate Bridge and the Oregon state line. Unlike most geothermal resources, the Geysers is a dry steam field which mainly produces superheated steam. Since October 16, 1997, the Geysers steam field has been recharged by injection of treated sewage effluent. Gravity and seismic studies suggest that the source of heat for the steam reservoir is a large magma chamber over 4 miles beneath the surface of the earth. For 12,000 years, Native American tribes built steam baths at the Geysers for cooking and healing purposes.

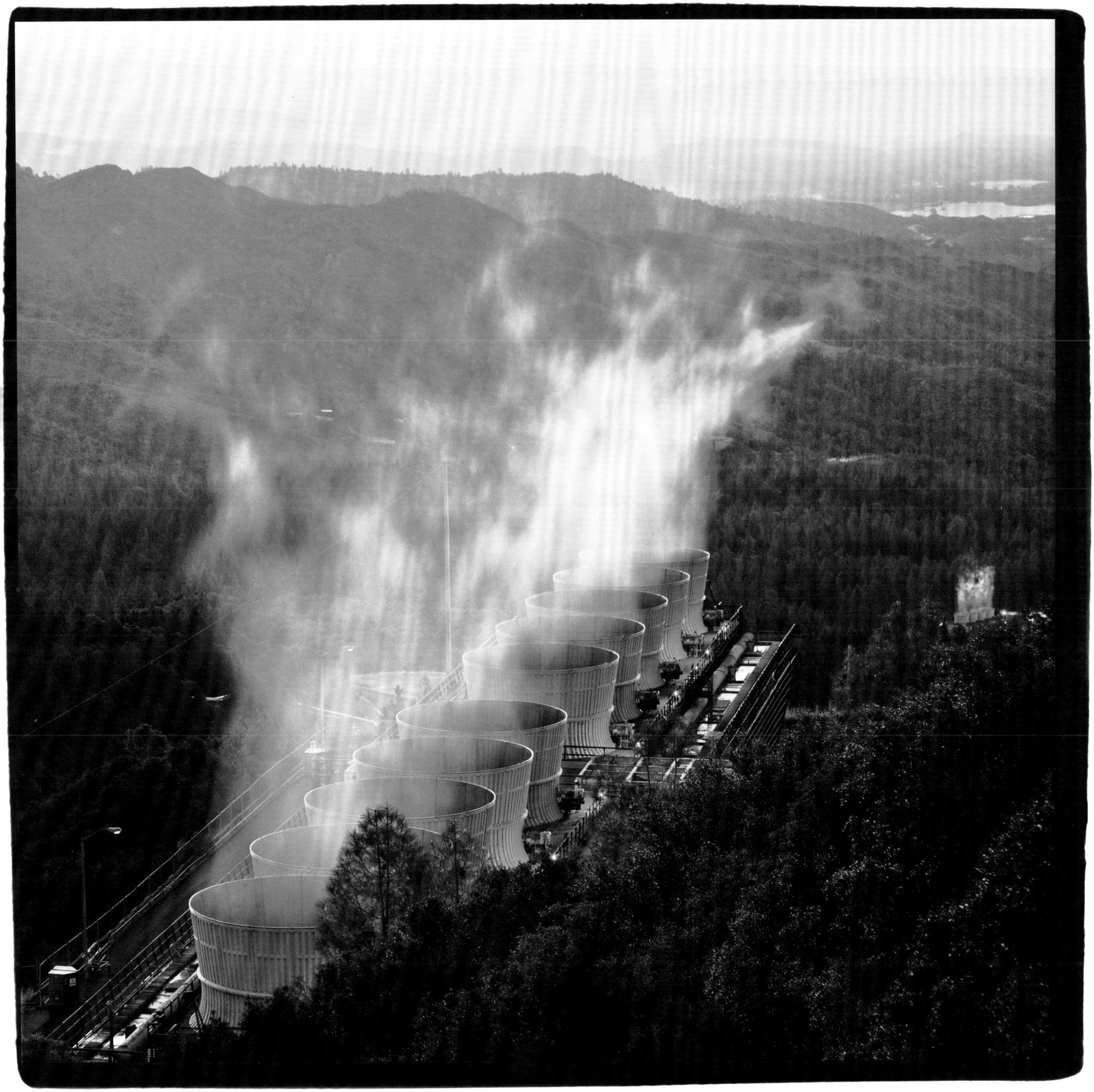

WIND ENERGY

Columbia River Gorge, Goodnoe Hills,
Washington
1983

The 80-mile gorge between Washington and Oregon amounts to a freeway for winds entering from the Pacific Ocean. These winds generate five gigawatts of electricity, more than twice the annual output of Hoover Dam. The pressure differential is caused by the colder moist air over Portland and the hot, dry air over the desert to the east of the Cascade Mountains. The cold air rushes toward the hot air to equalize that pressure, creating wind. Since 1975, NASA has managed a program for the US Department of Energy and the US Department of Interior to develop utility-scale wind turbines for electric power, in response to increasing oil prices. NASA designed and built its first prototype wind turbine, the 100 kW Mod-0 in Sandusky, Ohio, with funding from the National Science Foundation and ERDA. NASA and its contractors found that two blades can produce essentially equivalent energy as three blades but at a savings of the cost and weight of a blade, reducing the ratio in the gearbox. The Mod-0 was modeled after the lightweight two-bladed research turbine by Austrian Ulrich Hütter. This photograph is a Mod-2, 2,500 kW, 91-meter swept diameter turbine, produced by Boeing. Also photographed, for *LIFE Magazine*, was the WTS, 4,000 dW, 79.2-meter swept diameter turbine in Medicine Bow, WY, produced by United Technologies, which held the largest output record.

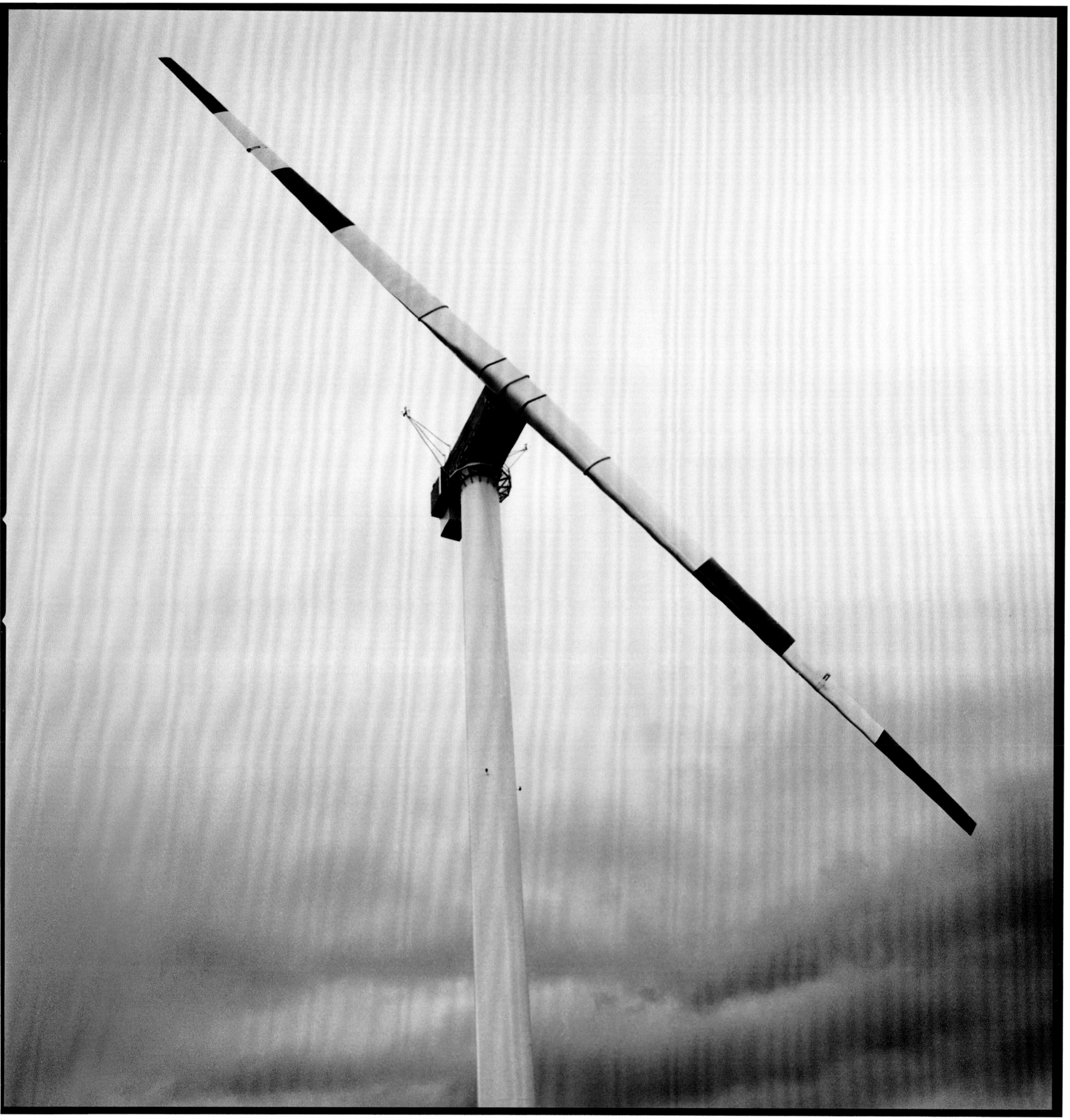

SWITCHING YARD

Hoover Dam, Boulder City, Nevada
1975

Hoover Dam was constructed between 1931 and 1936, during the Great Depression. Its main purposes were to harness the Colorado River to prevent periodic catastrophic flooding, to allocate and distribute water, and to generate hydroelectricity for the Southwest. At the time it was the world's largest project made with concrete, not to mention the largest public works project in US history. The dam's completion had a significant impact on Southern California, and in particular Los Angeles, since the power generated by the dam contributed to more than 70% of the city's power needs at the time. Excavation for the powerhouse at the dam's base was carried out simultaneously with the excavation for the dam's foundation and abutments. To make the powerhouse roof bombproof, it was constructed of layers of concrete, rock, and steel with a total thickness of about 3.5 feet, topped with layers of sand and tar. Shown here, sixteen high-voltage transmission lines connect Hoover Dam with its power market area. In total, there are 2,700 miles of transmission line cable sending electricity from Hoover Dam to Los Angeles. The power plant consists of 17 main Francis turbine generators and two Pelton wheel station service units (one for each plant wing). The total plant capacity is 2,079 MW. On October 9, 1936, the switch was thrown and electricity generated at the new Hoover Dam arrived in Los Angeles, which threw a big party. The "Light on Parade" proceeded down Broadway, nicknamed "the Canyon of Lights."

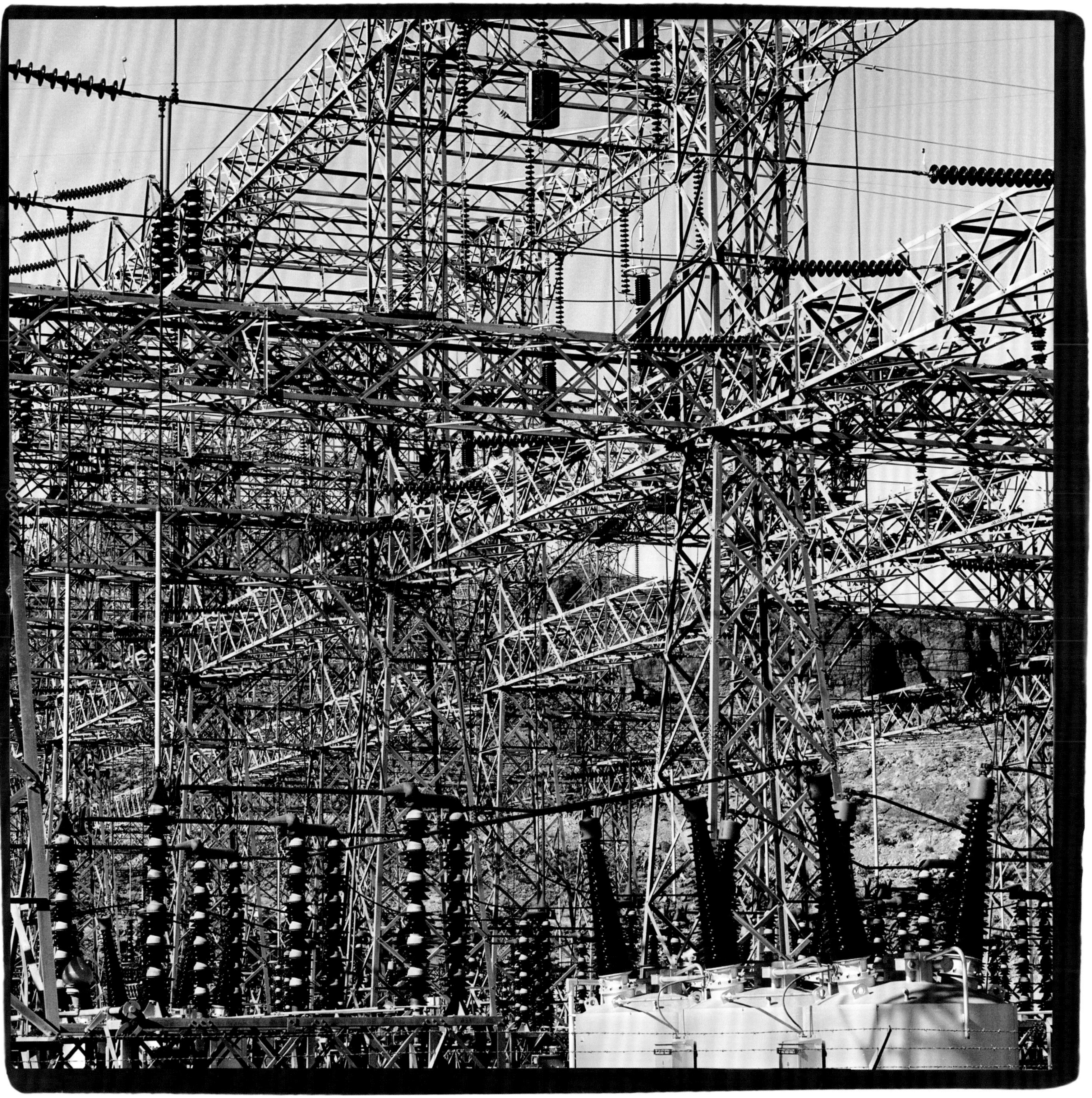

ROUGHNECKS

Oil Drilling, Permian Basin,
Texas
1984

John D. Rockefeller and his Standard Oil Company of Pennsylvania had an unchallenged historical monopoly on America's oil and gas supply. With significant oil strikes in Corsicana in 1894 and Spindletop's explosion in 1901, independent oil contractors, called wildcatters, soon stalked the Texas frontier looking for big bucks in the bubbling ground. Thousands of inexperienced farmers, called boll weevils, left their tractors and poured into boomtowns. Once they learned to sling heavy cables and pipes on the derrick floor, the farmers became oilmen and graduated to roughneck status. Roughneck specifically meant those who worked on the drill floor of a rig, handling specialized equipment for drilling and pressure controls. In oil fields, a roughneck's duties can include anything involved with connecting pipe down the well bore, as well as general work around a rig, which is what the men are doing here. They are connecting sections of pipes that are boring deep into the earth. Operating at high speeds and great friction, it is a very dangerous, laborious, and dirty job.

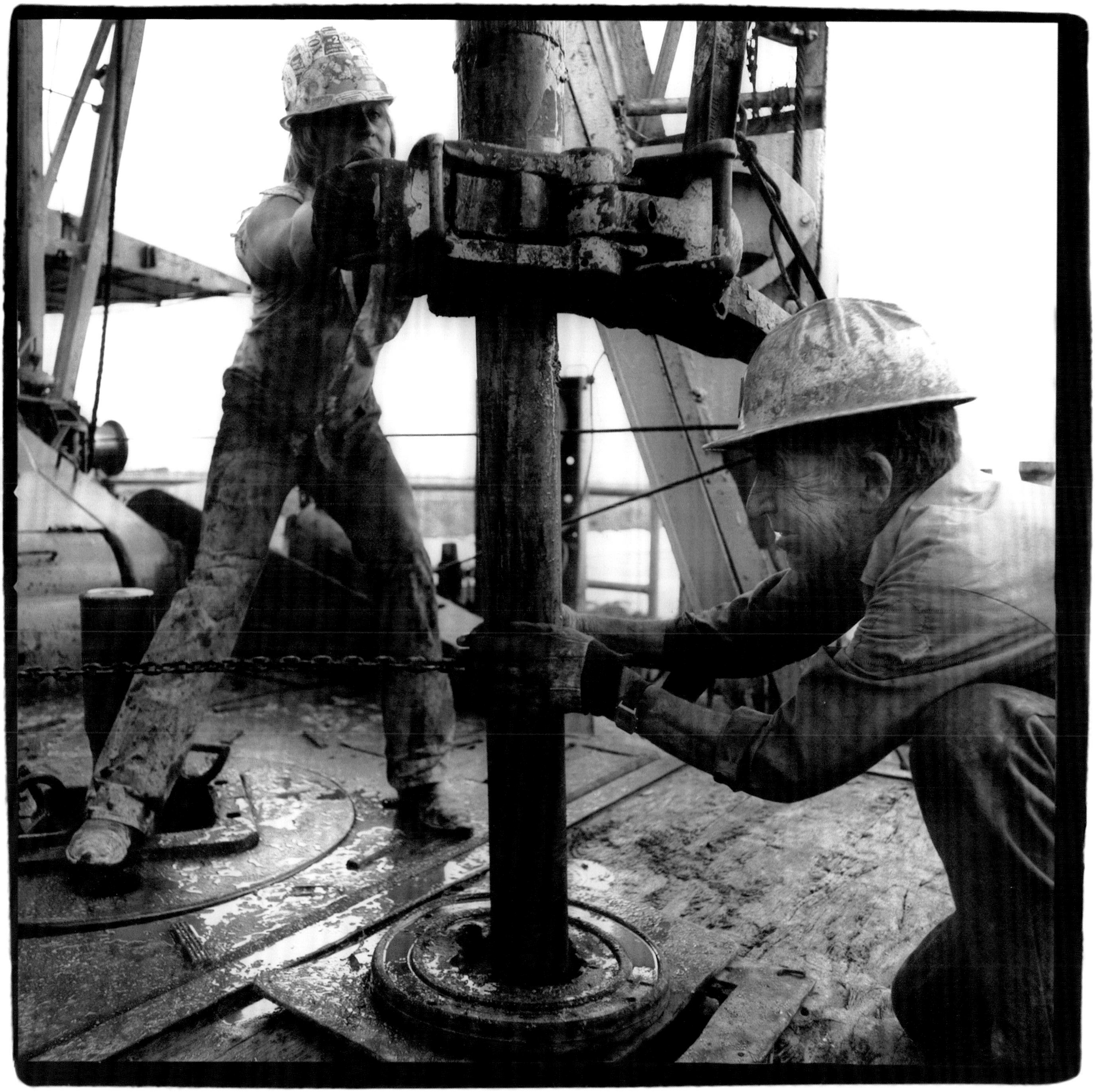

SPACE

ATLAS A BOOSTER

Cape Canaveral, Florida
1981

In 50 years of space history, more than 600 Atlas rockets have flown. Rocket designers in the 1950s faced challenges relating to weight. “Staging”—dropping of used engines and fuel tanks to lighten a rocket as it headed toward orbit—was the radical solution developed in which the inner engine (the sustainer engine) remained permanently attached to the rocket, while the two outer engines (booster engines) were used only during the first few minutes of flight. By shedding the weight of the two boosters, the Atlas was light enough to fly all the way to orbit using only the sustainer engine. Another design feature of the Atlas, a “balloon” structure, was so lightweight that the fuel tanks needed to be continuously pressurized to avoid collapsing under their own weight. The balloon structure, and the ability to drop the booster engines in flight, allowed the Atlas to start and test all main engines while still safely on the ground. From 1962 to 1963, Atlas booster launched the first four US astronauts to orbit the Earth. Variations of the craft launched 63 times between 1991 and 2004. The Atlas V is still in service. More than 600 launches have been accomplished

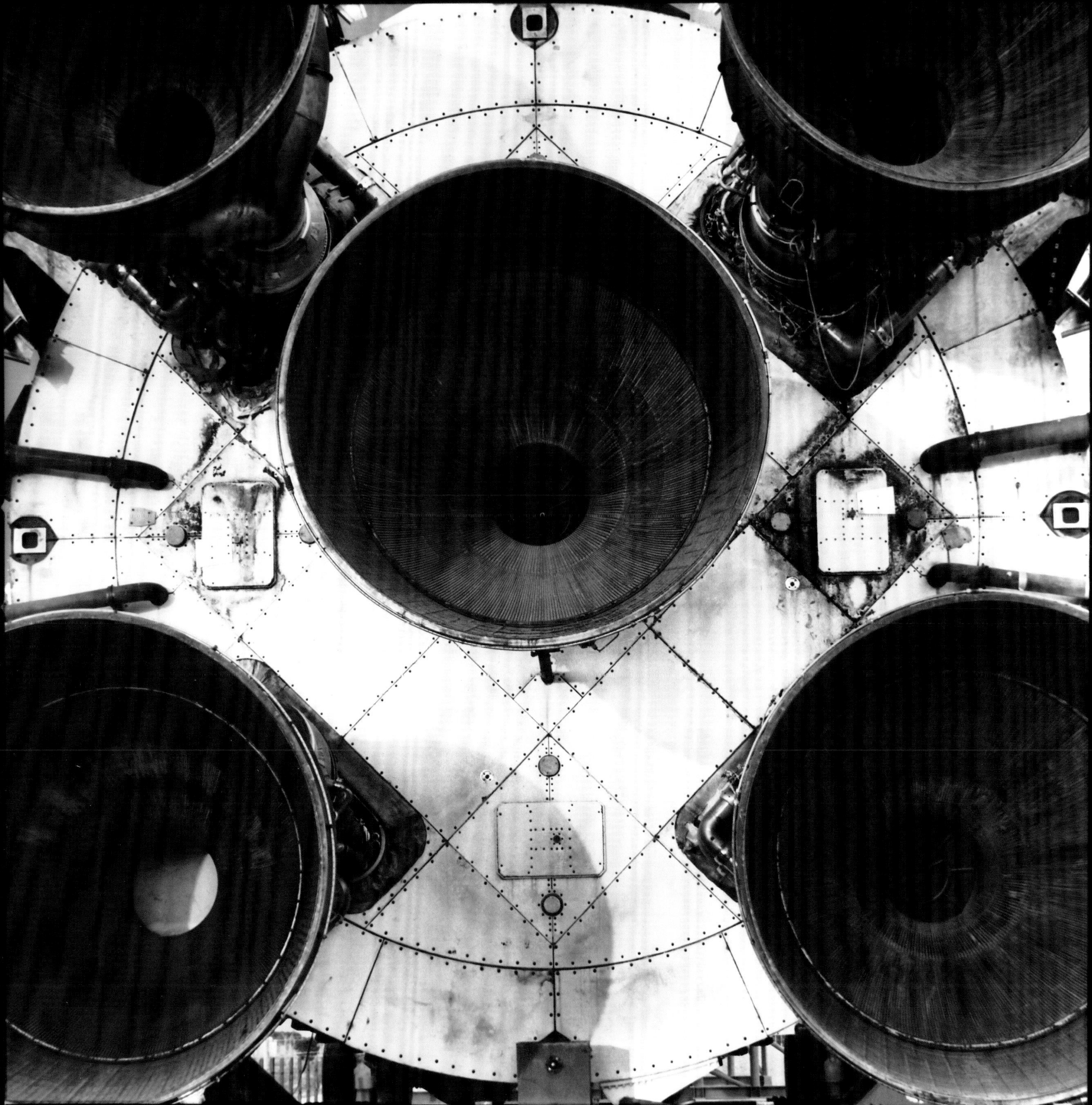

HUBBLE TELESCOPE

Clean Room, Lockheed,
Sunnyvale, California
1986

Hubble, the observatory, was the first major optical telescope to be placed in space. Even though initially impaired by a flaw in its main mirror attributed to manufacturer Perkin Elmer, it launched in 1990. The 12.5-ton orbiting observatory was repaired in 1993 in space. Far above rain, clouds, and light pollution, Hubble has an unobstructed view of the universe. Hubble's launch and deployment in April 1990 marked the most significant advance in astronomy since Galileo's telescope. The clean room (photographed here in California) is one of the elaborate steps that are vital to the success of every Hubble mission. Even a speck of dust or a fingerprint could severely damage the sensitive components. The expensive project was a tough sell, but NASA upped their lobbying efforts and got buy-in from the European Space Agency, which shared the costs. The Large Space Telescope was renamed the Hubble (HST) in honor of Edwin Hubble, an American astronomer who, among other things, determined that the universe extended beyond the borders of the Milky Way. The telescope continues to contribute to astrophysics today.

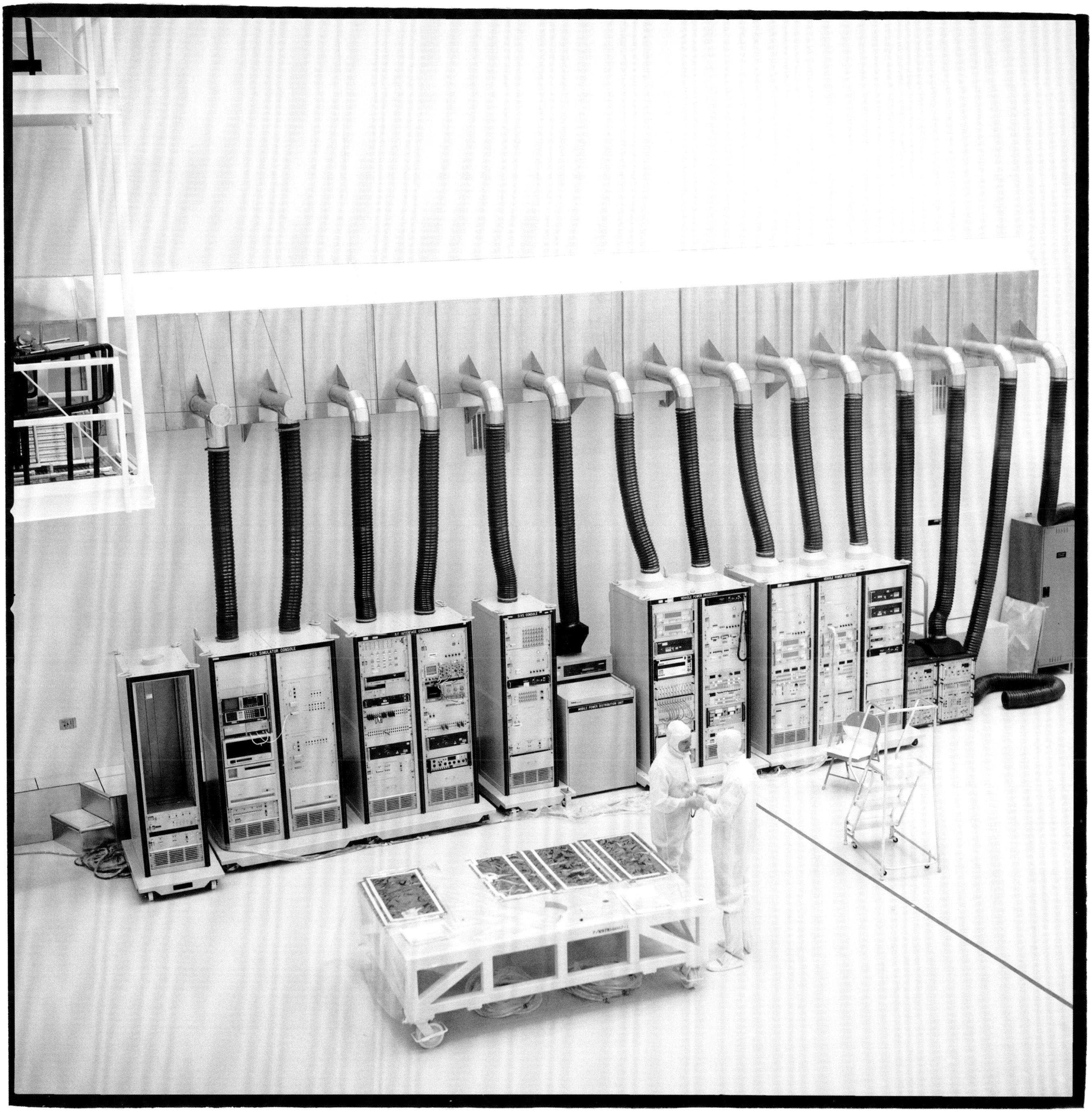
PCS SIMULATOR CONSOLE
VEHICLE POWER PROCESSOR
MOBILE POWER DISTRIBUTION UNIT
VEHICLE POWER INTERFACE

NASA WIND TUNNEL

Plum Brook Station,
Cleveland, Ohio
1991

The Hypersonic Tunnel Facility (HTF) at NASA's Plum Brook Station was originally designed to test nuclear thermal rocket nozzles. Utilized to conduct research, development, and acceptance testing of hypersonic air breathing propulsion systems, the Hypersonic Tunnel Facility is a fully self-contained facility; a blow-down, non-vitiated, free jet wind tunnel that is capable of simulating Mach 5, Mach 6, and Mach 7 true enthalpy conditions. Due to the high-energy nature of the facility, it is operated remotely from a control room approximately one-quarter mile from the actual facility. The test section is voluminous enough to accommodate large-scale models and full-size aircraft constituents. Hypersonic weapons present one of the greatest threats to US national security today. The ability to travel at ultra-high velocity is the primary appeal of hypersonic missiles because it extends their range and allows them to bypass modern layered missile defenses. Plum Brook Station has large, unique facilities that simulate the environment of space.

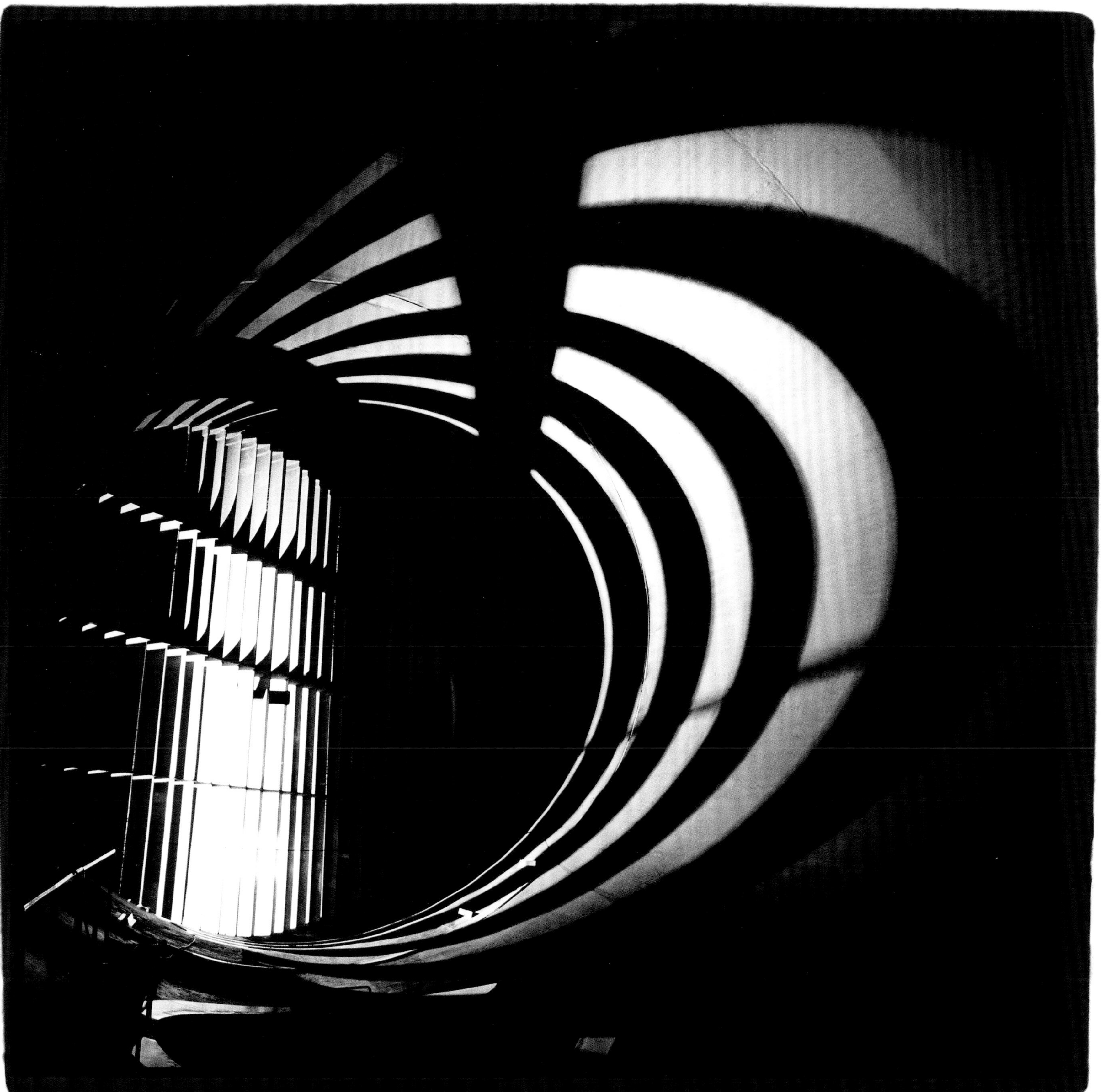

COLLIMATED MIRROR

JAXA's Tsukuba Space Center (TKSC),
Japan
1994

The Tsukuba Space Center, also known by its radio call sign Tsukuba, is the operations facility and headquarters for the Japan Aerospace Exploration Agency. The TKSC facility serves as the primary location for Japan's space operations and research programs. A collimator is a device that narrows a beam of particles or waves. Narrowing causes the directions of motion to become more aligned in a narrowed, specific focus. The mirror testing facility, located in a room the size of a football field, is designed to collimate laser beams of light on honeycombed shaped mirrors to simulate the intensity of the sun while the spacecraft is rotating in outer space. The range of heat and cold could be as much as 500 degrees Celsius, which applies great tensile dynamics on the materials of the craft. Gold foil is often used in satellites because of its expansion and contraction qualities. There is an older and smaller version of one other such mirror, at the Jet Propulsion Laboratory (JPL) in Pasadena, CA.

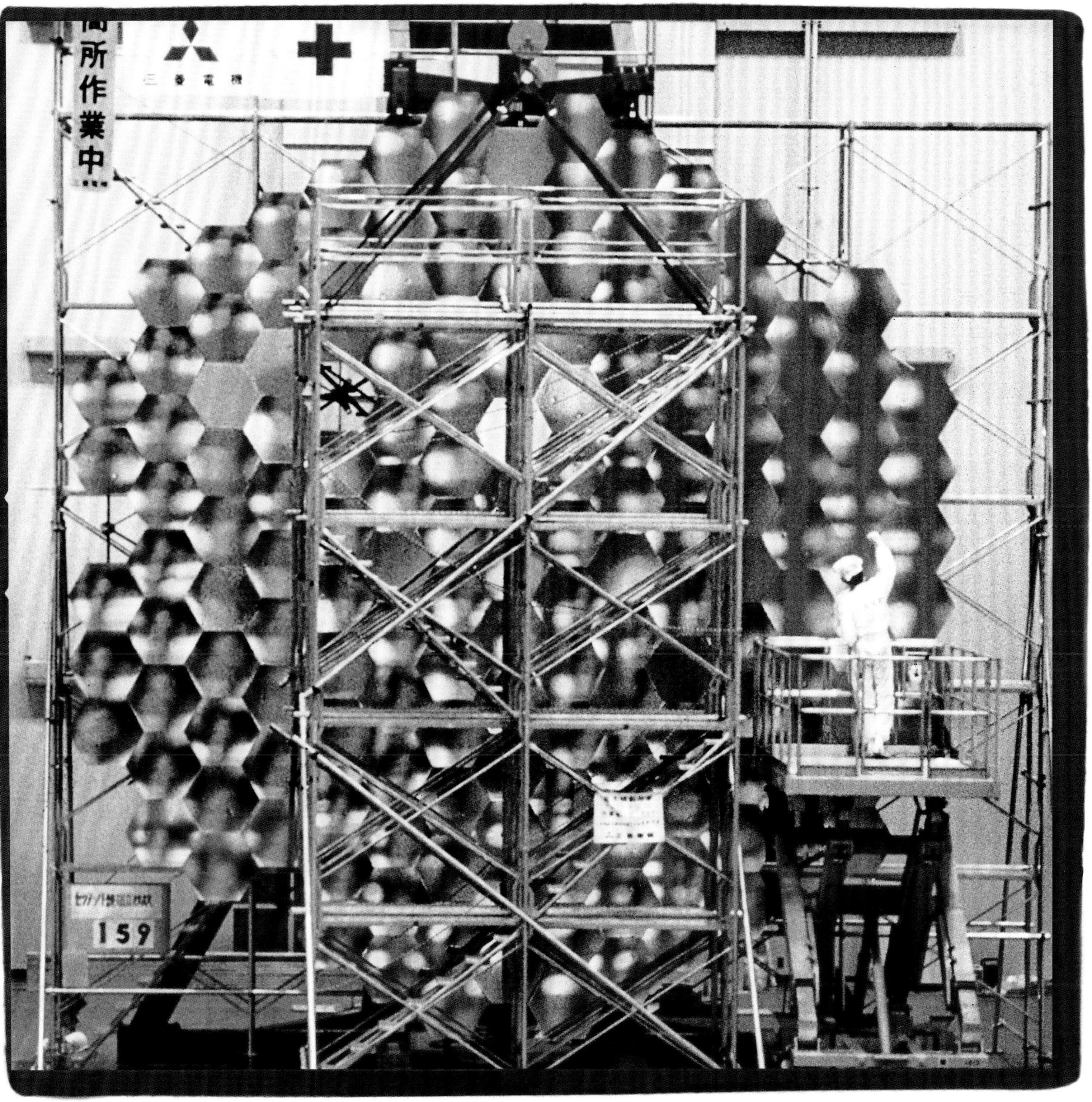
所作業中
三菱電機
159

LARGE FORMAT CAMERA

Johnson Space Center,
Houston, Texas
1984

The Large Format Camera (LFC) was a photographic camera with a 305-mm focal length, an F/6 aperture, and a film format of 23 by 46 cm. The objective was to evaluate the utility of orbital photography for cartographic mapping and land use studies at scales of 1:50,000. Its cost was estimated at US$11.4 million. It was launched on the Challenger Space Shuttle before its accident. On October 5, 1984, nearly 20 years after it was conceived, the LFCIARS was finally carried into space on Shuttle Mission STS-41G. Requests for coverage had been received for 368 sites located on all continents except Antarctica. Optically, mechanically, and electrically, the camera operated without flaw, and many exceptional scenes were captured. The primary purpose of the Large Format Camera, which was a major component of the Orbiter Camera Payload System, was to enhance worldwide topographic mapping precision with high-resolution space photography. However, NASA was not successful in interesting other agencies or private companies in paying the costs to use it on the shuttle, so it only made the one flight.

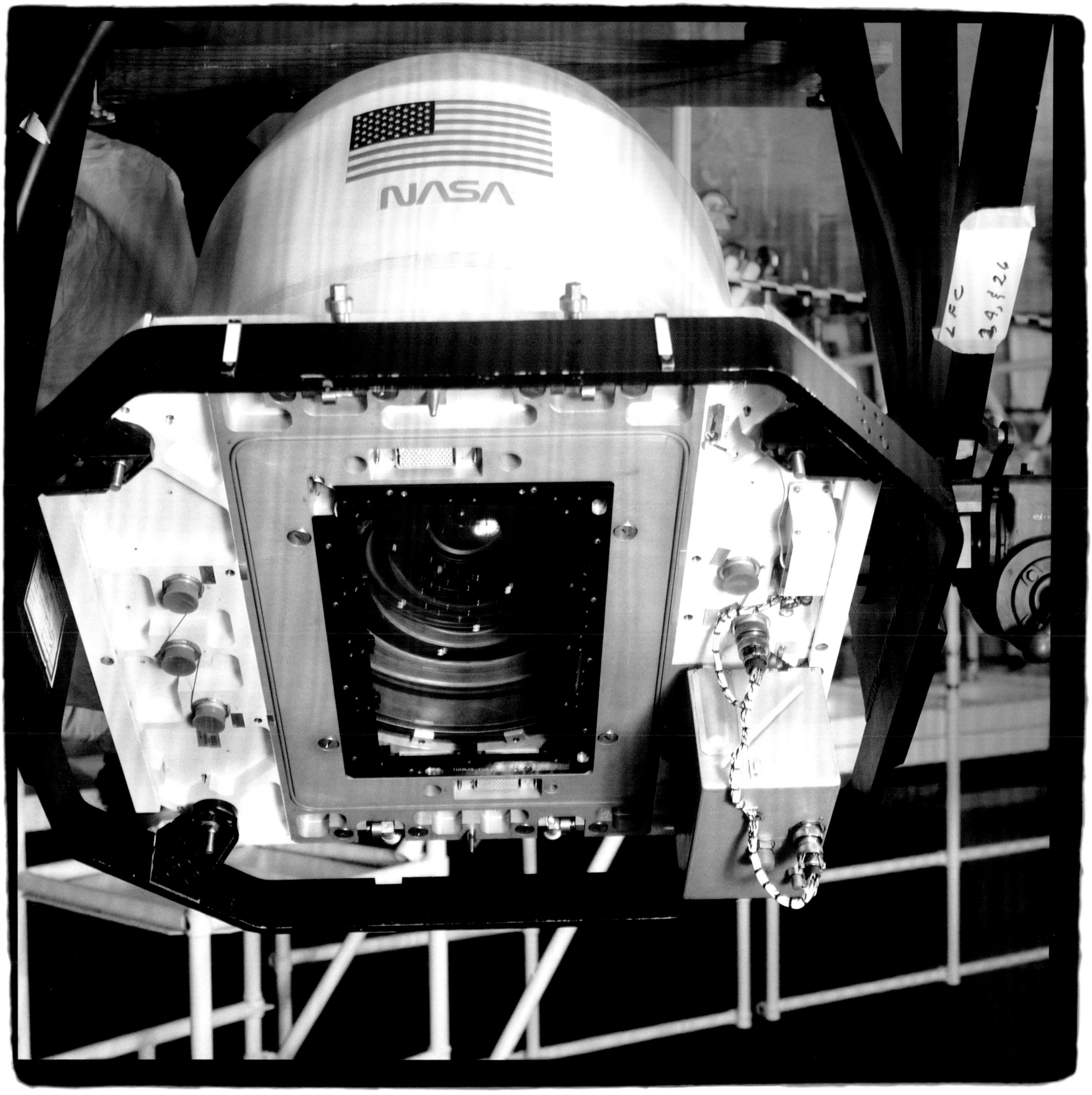
NASA
LFC

THERMAL VACUUM CHAMBER

Ford Aerospace,
El Segundo, California
1983

Thermal vacuum chambers are ideal for testing spacecraft components in a simulated space environment. Not only do they enable spacecraft components to be tested in a space-like vacuum, but they also allow component performance to be assessed under varying temperatures. The fundamental purpose of thermal vacuum testing is to understand the satellite's performance through environmental extremes and thus increase mission assurance through a test-like-you-fly environment. A thermal vacuum chamber is a radiative thermal controlled environment. Typically the thermal environment is achieved by passing liquids or fluids through thermal shrouds for cold temperatures, or through the application of thermal lamps for high temperatures. Thermal analyses are conducted on the design using thermal models, which are then verified and tested. This was the case here in my photograph, testing a telecommunications satellite. It stands five stories tall.

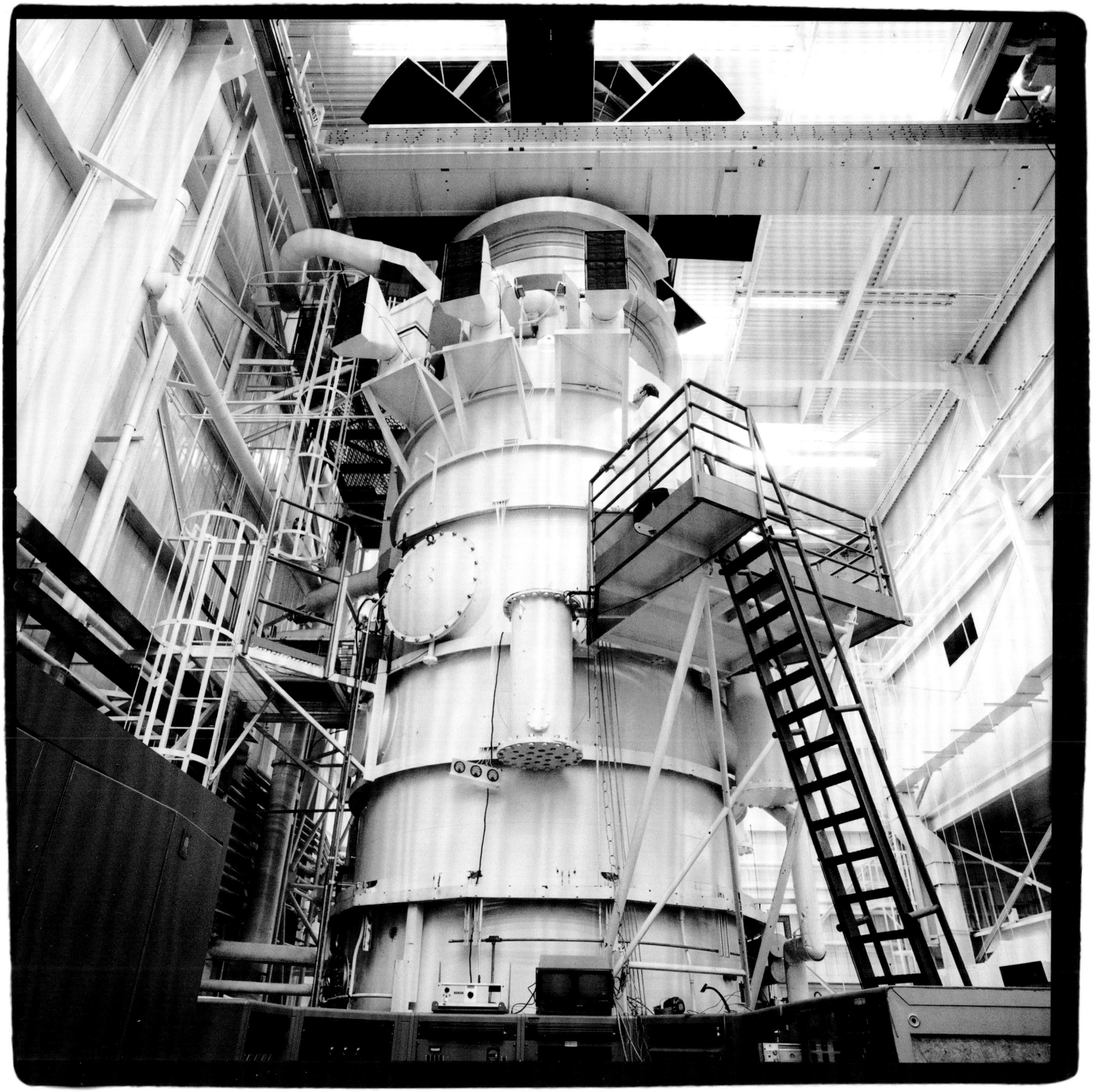

INTERNATIONAL SPACE STATION (ISS)

Cape Canaveral, Florida
1998

The International Space Station (ISS) is a modular space station (habitable artificial satellite) in low Earth orbit. The ISS program is a multi-national collaborative project between five participating space agencies: NASA (US), Roscosmos (Russia), JAXA (Japan), ESA (Europe), and CSA (Canada). Its main construction was completed between 1998 and 2011, although the station continually evolves to include new missions and experiments. It has been continuously occupied since November 2, 2000. Astronaut time and research time on the space station is allocated to space agencies relative to how much money or resources (such as modules or robotics) they contribute. The ISS serves as a microgravity and space environment research laboratory in which scientific experiments are conducted in astrobiology, astronomy, meteorology, physics, and other fields. The ISS is a platform for long-term research for human health, which NASA bills as a key stepping-stone to letting humans explore other solar system destinations such as the moon or Mars. It is the largest artificial object in space and the largest satellite in low Earth orbit, regularly visible to the naked eye from Earth's surface. The station is expected to operate until 2030.

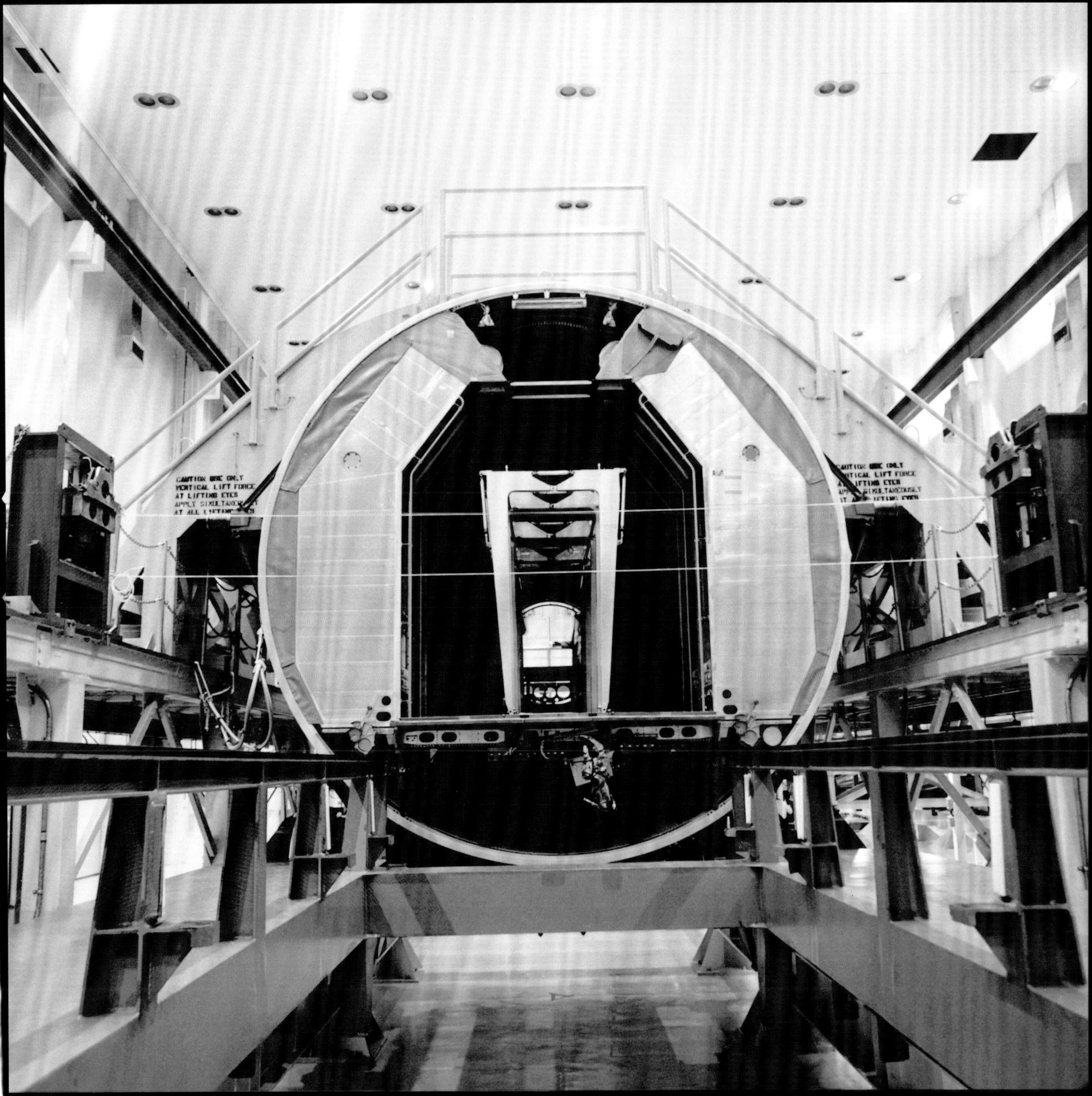
CAUTION USE ONLY
VERTICAL LIFT FORCE
AT LIFTING EYES

SATELLITE, FUEL CELL

Hughes Aerospace,
Los Angeles, California
1984

The Hughes Aircraft Company was a major American aerospace and defense contractor founded in 1932, by Howard Hughes, as a division of Hughes Tool Company. A fuel cell is an electrochemical cell that converts the chemical energy of a fuel (often hydrogen) and an oxidizing agent (often oxygen) into electricity through a pair of redox reactions. Fuel cells are different from most batteries in requiring a continuous source of fuel and oxygen to sustain the chemical reaction, whereas in a battery the chemical energy usually comes from metals and their ions or oxides that are commonly already present in the battery, except in flow batteries. Fuel cells can produce electricity continuously for as long as fuel and oxygen are supplied. The first fuel cells were invented by Sir William Grove in 1838. The first commercial use of fuel cells came a century later, following the invention of the hydrogen–oxygen fuel cell by Francis Thomas Bacon in 1932. The alkaline fuel cell, also known as the Bacon fuel cell after its inventor, has been used in NASA space programs since the mid-1960s to generate power for satellites and space capsules.

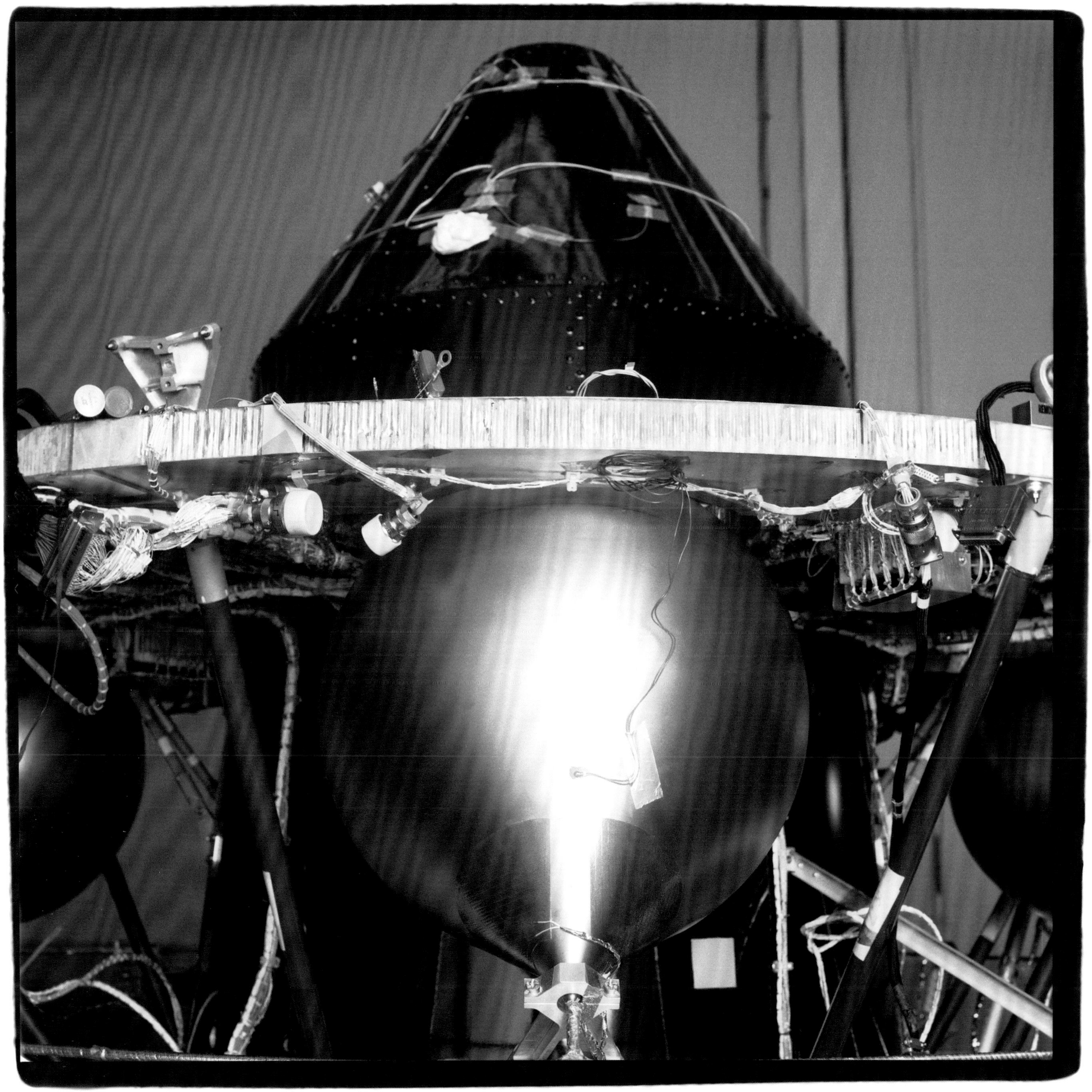

CHALLENGER SPACE SHUTTLE

Cape Canaveral, Florida
1986

Challenger, launched as the 25th Space Shuttle Program flight (and the craft's 10th mission), climbed quickly and gracefully into the crystal clear Florida sky. At 11:39:13 EST on January 28, 1986, the space shuttle broke apart 73 seconds into its flight, killing all seven crew members aboard. Challenger was, at the time, the most-flown orbiter in NASA's fleet, having risen quickly to prominence as the fleet leader in terms of not only the number of missions flown, but also its impressive scientific and technological accomplishments. Challenger was the workhorse of the early days of the shuttle fleet, setting numerous records and leaving behind a legacy of education and inspiration. Beginning life as STA-099 (Structural Test Article-099), the components that would eventually become the airframe and body for orbiter Challenger were initially used by the Space Shuttle Program (SSP) to test and validate the effects of launch and entry stress. In all, Space Shuttle Challenger deployed nine satellites, spending a total of 62 days 7 hours 56 minutes and traveling 25,803,936 miles in 995 orbits of Earth.

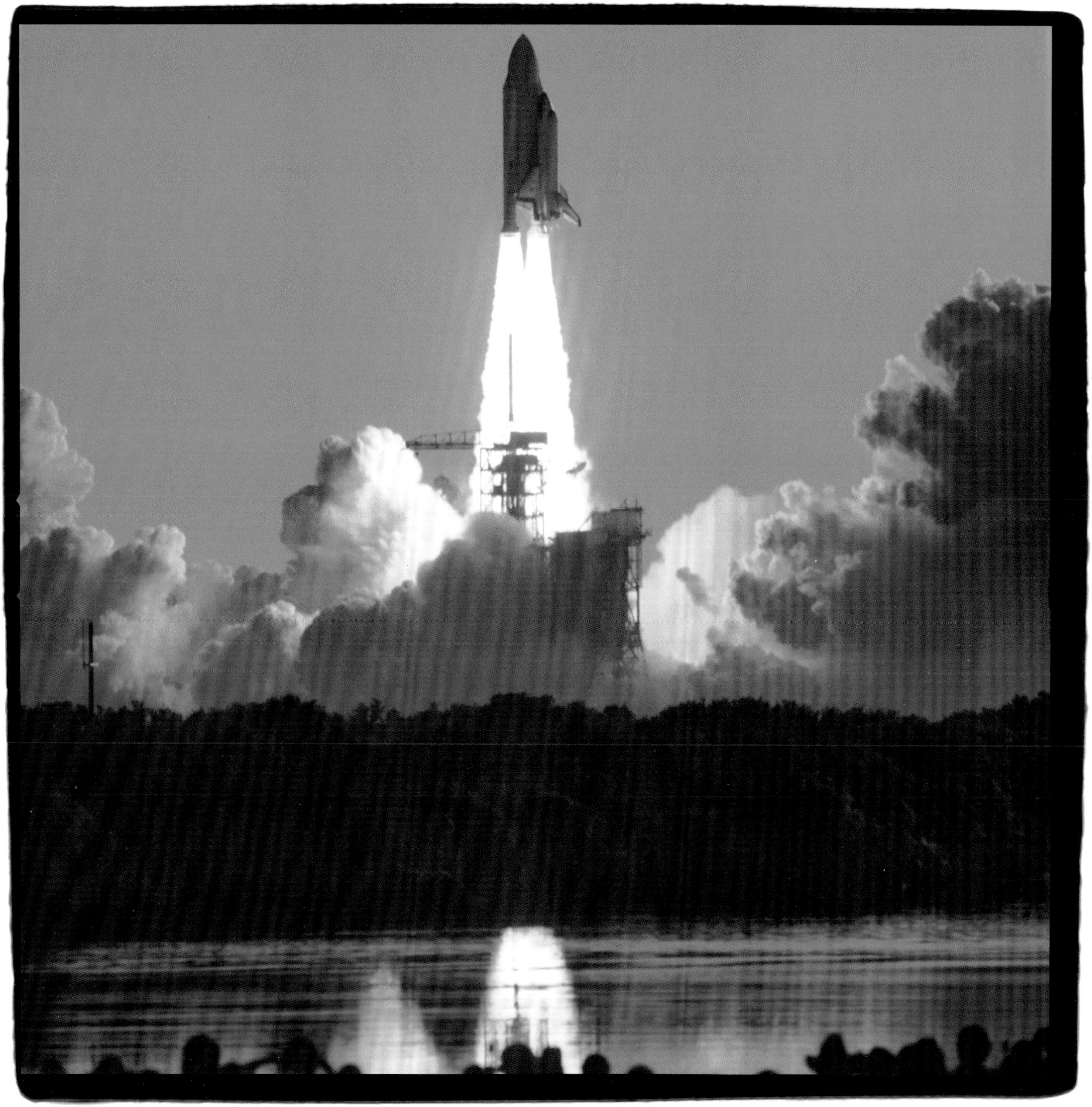

HEAVY INDUSTRY

BETHLEHEM STEEL FACTORY

Seattle, Washington
1975

Bethlehem Steel Corporation, a cultural icon named after a town in Pennsylvania, was an American steel and shipbuilding company that for much of the twentieth century was one of the world's largest steel producing and shipbuilding companies. The company was founded in 1857 as the Saucona Iron Company. Production in the early days fed the American skyscraper industry, making standardized frames for the tall buildings. The Bethlehem Steel Corporation and the Bethlehem Shipbuilding Corporation were two of the most powerful symbols of American industrial manufacturing leadership. Established in 1904 in West Seattle, the Bethlehem Steel Factory (shown here) produced enough steel to manufacture 250 destroyers in a year. This photograph is of one of Bethlehem's three rolling mills where red hot ingots were transformed into long bars. By the middle of the twentieth century the Bethlehem Steel Corporation produced 23 million tons of steel per year. This massive growth in production was a result of the destroyed plants in Germany and Japan during the Second World War. The demise of Bethlehem Steel Corporation in 1995 is often cited as one of the most prominent examples of the US economy's shift away from industrial manufacturing, its failure to compete with global competition, and management's penchant for short-term profits

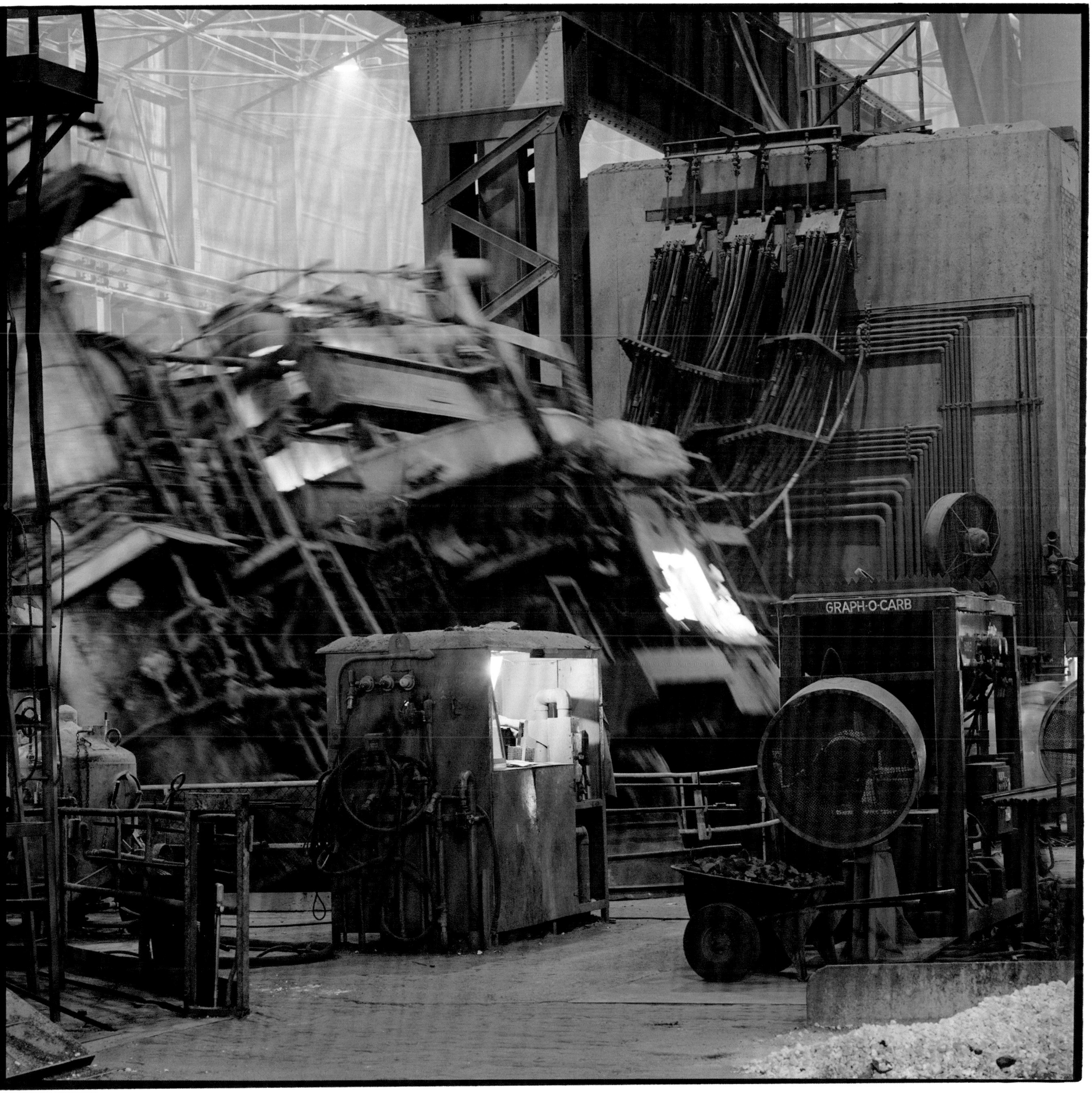
GRAPH-O-CARB

ANCHOR, CONTAINER SHIP

Harbor Island, Seattle, Washington
1976

Seattle historically relied on its location on a "great-circle" route to Asia, to maintain its competitiveness with larger West Coast ports. Container shipping was introduced in the 1950s, with the first modern container ships coming to Seattle in the mid-1960s. By the 1970s, containerization demanded acres of space for container storage, required fewer longshore workers, and greatly reduced the time ships spent in the harbor. This led to drastic changes in pier operations and longshore working conditions. The Port of Seattle is the fifth largest container port in the US, and the twentieth largest in the world. Served by 24 regularly scheduled shipping lines, it is the top US port in container tonnage exports to Asia. Economic impact to the region exceeds a total of 45,500 jobs, US$3.2 billion in labor income, and US$9.7 billion in business output. Built by Puget Sound Bridge and Dredging Company, Harbor Island was completed in 1909 at the Duwamish River, where it empties into Elliott Bay. At the time of completion it was the largest artificial island in the world at 350 acres.

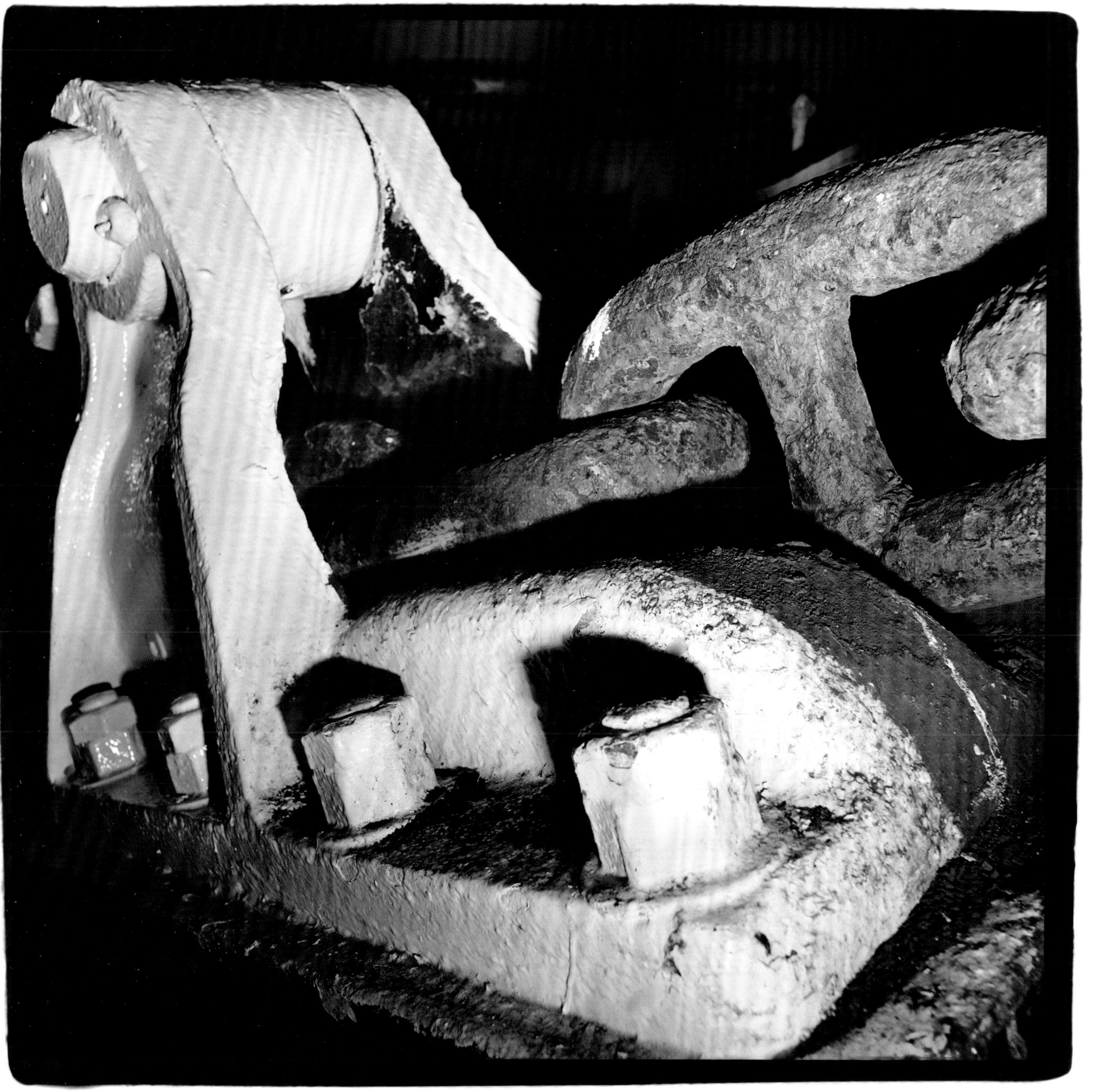

SHIP BUILDING

Newport News, Virginia
1985

Northrop Grumman Shipbuilding built small ships, supercarriers, and submarines. Today, Newport News Shipbuilding (which merged with Northrup Grumman) is the largest industrial employer in Virginia. The sole designer, builder, and refueler of US Navy aircraft carriers, and one of two providers of US Navy submarines, it is located close to a massive naval base. Founded as the Chesapeake Dry Dock and Construction Co. in 1886, Newport News Shipbuilding has built more than 800 ships. In 2013, the company began the deactivation of the first nuclear-powered aircraft carrier, USS Enterprise, which it also built. Newport News Shipbuilding also performs refueling and complex overhaul work on Nimitz-class aircraft carriers. The yard has completed four Nimitz-class carriers (USS Nimitz, USS Dwight D. Eisenhower, USS Carl Vinson, and USS Theodore Roosevelt). Work is underway for the fifth Nimitz-class vessel, USS Abraham Lincoln, and a sixth Nimitz-class vessel, USS George Washington. In January 2018, the facility lifted and mounted a 400-metric-ton, 80-foot-high watertight “caisson unit” into its Joint Manufacturing Assembly Facility, revolutionizing how submarines are built.

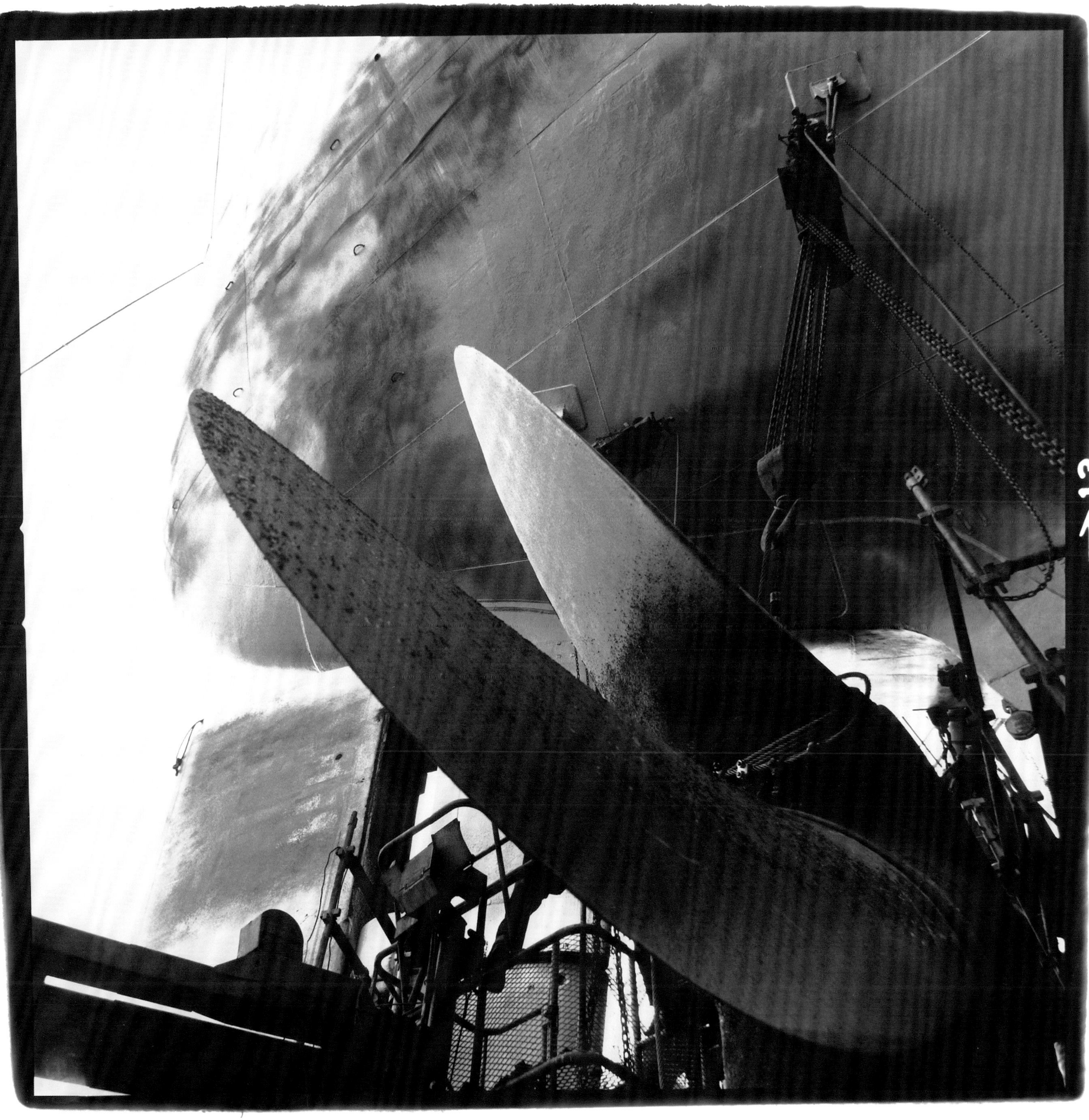

IBM BUILDING

New York, New York
1980

Designed by Edward Larrabee Barnes & Associates in the early 1980s, the overhanging, unsupported skyscraper corner above Madison Avenue and 57th Street required the largest single piece of steel ever erected. The construction of this new IBM building is a wedge-shaped structure in glass and greenish-black granite. The large airy atrium was designed by landscape architect Robert Zion. The transparent trapezoidal atrium projects from the building toward 56th Street, offering a public outdoor plaza. A red Alexander Calder sculpture floats inside. Green bamboo trees evoke the serenity of an indoor garden. The granite paving extends into the lobby, where it is met by a dramatic Michael Heizer horizontal granite fountain. The original building that stood at the site was built in 1938 for IBM and was demolished in 1977. Six years later, the new building replaced it, twice the size of its original. IBM owned the building until 1994, when it was then sold to the Odyssey Corporation. The new owners kept the IBM logo on the building's entrance, and most people still refer to it as the IBM building. IBM remains a major tenant in the building.

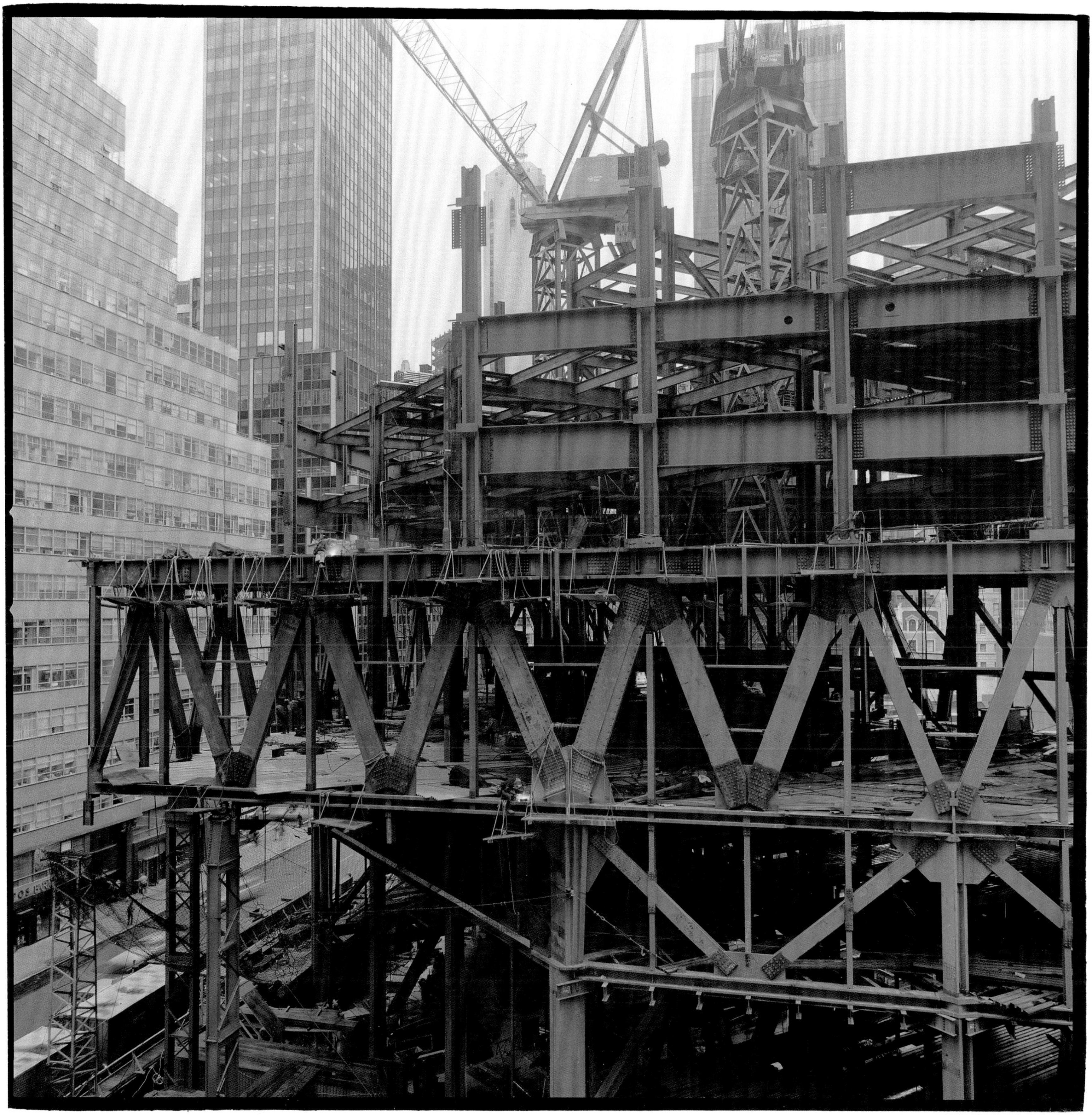

WASHINGTON, D.C. METRO

Dupont Circle, Washington, D.C.
1986

The idea for a rail system in the nation's capital was born in the 1950s. Washington's Metro system opened to great fanfare in 1976. The initial line included just five stations stretching from Farragut North to Rhode Island Avenue. De Leuw, Cather & Company worked out the engineering, Bechtel Corporation handled construction, and Harry Weese & Associates designed the architecture. Weese's clean and monumental design aimed to be the antithesis of New York's subway, with its graffiti, low ceilings, and industrial appearance. Weese proposed vaults, turning stations into underground equivalents of classic nineteenth-century rail stations, with their cast-iron train sheds, but with concrete. Vaults allowed him to dispense with columns, improving sightlines and giving stations a sense of spaciousness. The Metro is one of the largest public-works projects ever built and one of the busiest rail transit systems in the US. Photographed here, Dupont Circle station opened on January 17, 1977, the first to open after the original stretch of the Red Line. The poured drop formed concrete design created a dramatic, futuristic station, but it is difficult to clean. It houses a grand entrance escalator topped with a circular arch that contains the immortal words of "The Wound-Dresser" by Walt Whitman, published in *Drum-Taps* in 1865. It starts with, *"Thus in silence in dreams' projections ..."*

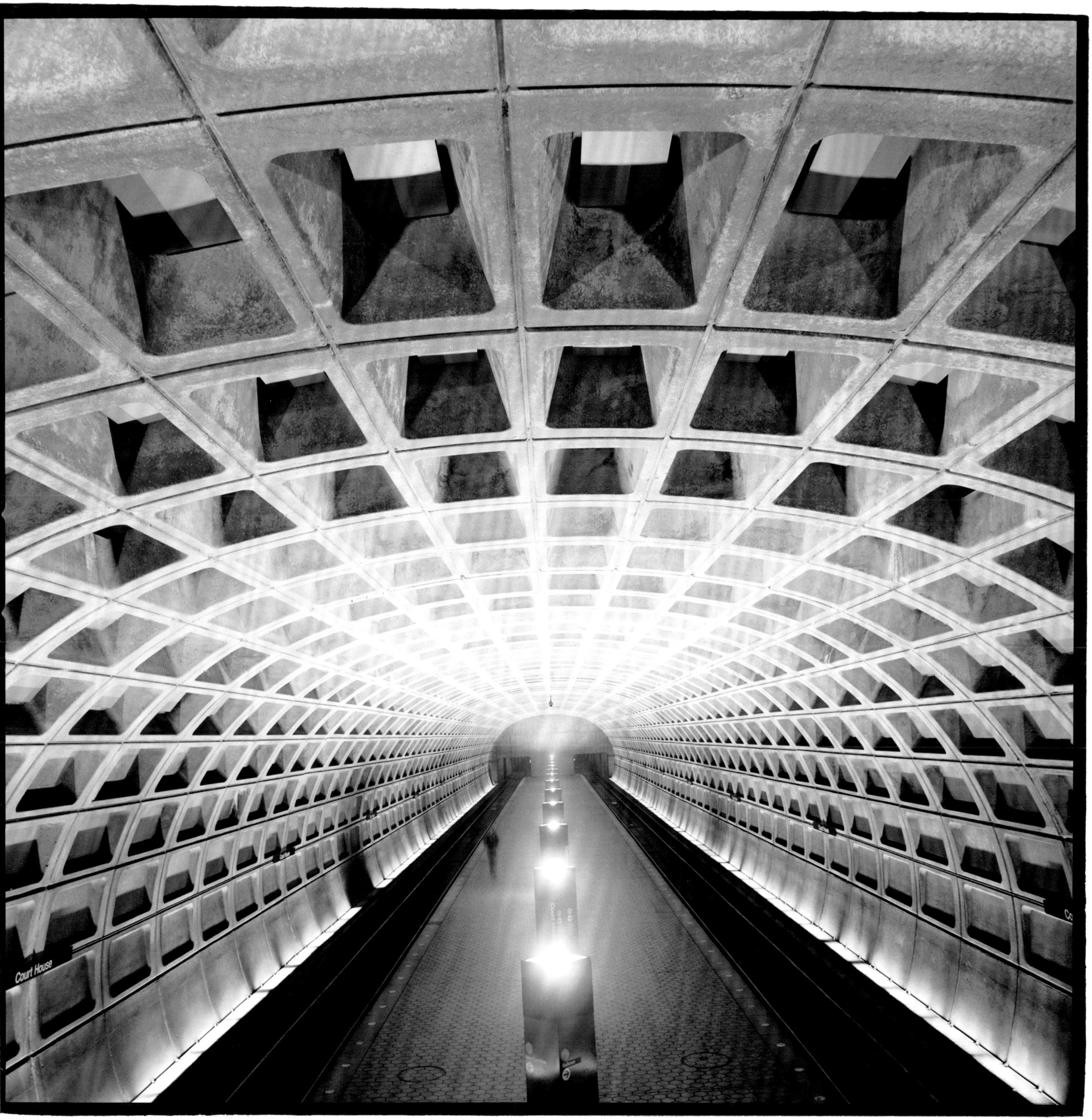
Court House

THE FORD RIVER ROUGE COMPLEX

Dearborn, Michigan
1997

Construction of the River Rouge Complex began in 1917, was completed in 1928, and inspired the GAZ factory, built in the 1930s in the Soviet Union. Designed by Albert Kahn, the Rouge was designated as a National Historic Landmark District in 1978. The Rouge includes 93 buildings, 16 million square feet of factory floor space, docks, 100 miles of interior railroad track, an electricity plant, and an integrated steel mill. The titanic Rouge was able to turn raw materials into running vehicles within this single complex. More than 100,000 workers were employed there, even during the 1930s Great Depression. Mexican artist Diego Rivera captured Rouge in a set of murals known as *Detroit Industry.* The Rouge's first products were Eagle Boats. In 1927, automobile production began, with the Ford Model A. A labor union attempted to form in 1937, but was beaten down by management. During World War II, Rouge produced jeeps, aircraft engines, aircraft components, tires, tubes, armor plates, and tractors. This photograph is of the dismantling of the original plant, photographed for *Fortune Magazine.* In 1999, William McDonough redesigned the 85-year-old, 1,212-acre River Rouge facility, which features a vegetation-covered roof and rainwater reclamation system. This facility is still Ford's largest factory and employs 6,000 workers.

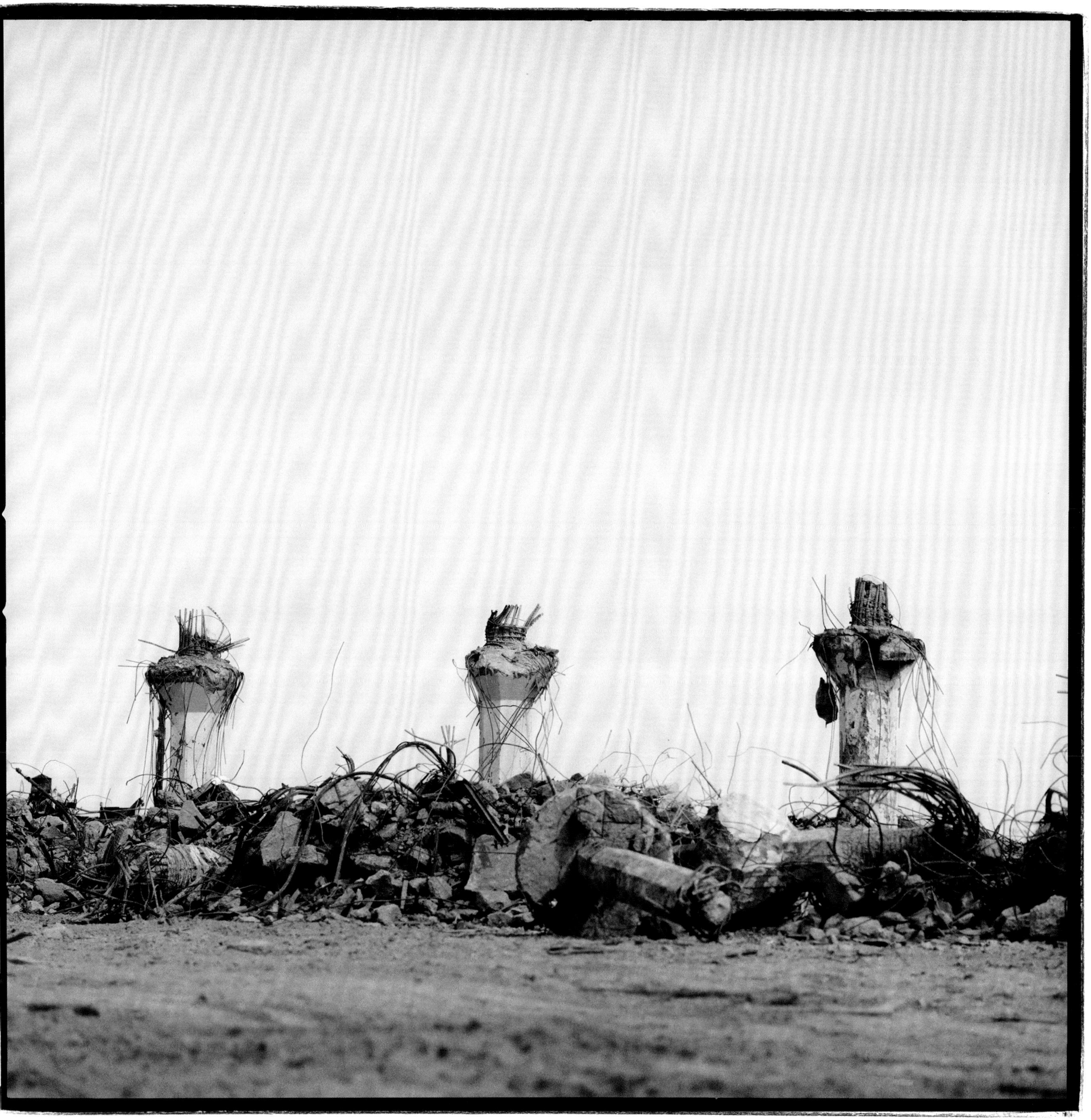

MAERSK SUPER CONTAINER SHIPS

Long Beach, California
2015

The Maersk Triple E-class container ships comprise a family of very large container ships of more than 18,000 TEU, capable of carrying 2,500 more containers. Built at 1,310 feet and costing US$190 million per ship, they were the largest container ships in the world. The Triple-E name is derived from the class's three-E design principles: economy of scale, energy efficiency, and environmental improvement. They are too wide to traverse the Panama Canal, but can pass through the Suez Canal. The dual 39,800hp ultra-long stroke two-stroke diesel engines drive two propellers at 19 knots. This class is by design slower than its predecessors, using a strategy known as slow steaming to lower fuel consumption by 37% and carbon dioxide emissions by 50%. The Triple-E design won Maersk a Sustainable Ship Operator of the Year award. They were built by Daewoo Shipbuilding & Marine Engineering; the initial 10-ship order was valued at US$1.9 billion. Maersk employs the ships to service routes between Europe and Asia, which represents the company's largest market. Over 100 ships serve this route, limited only by shore-side equipment in the ports for loading and offloading.

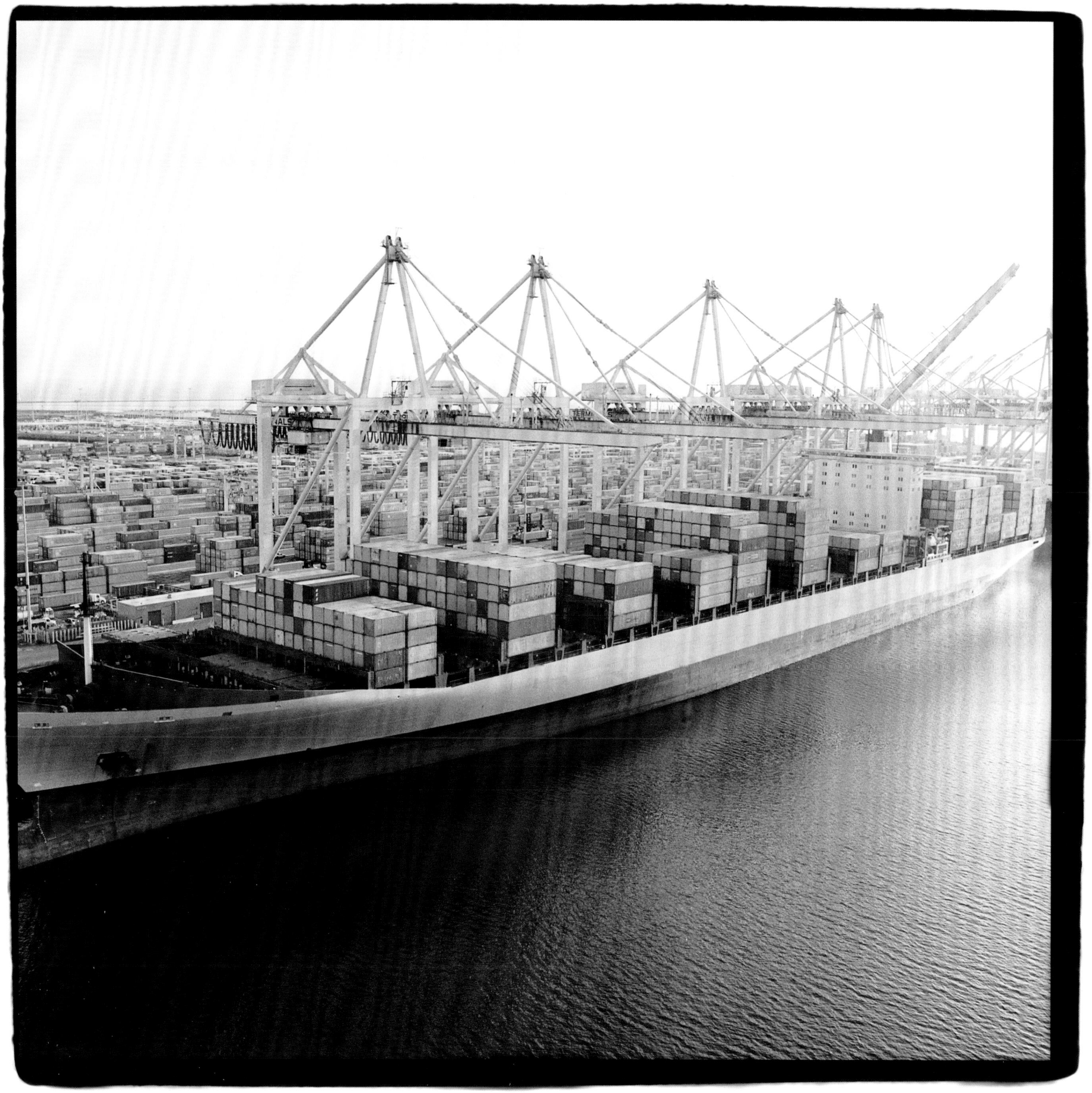

WHEAT SHIPPING BY RAIL

Saskatchewan, Canada
2005

Canadian commercial production of spring wheat started with the first recorded attempt at growing wheat in present-day Saskatchewan by the French in the Carrot River Valley sometime between 1753 and 1756. Wheat rapidly became the most important crop grown in Saskatchewan with four million hectares planted by 1919. The majority of the wheat produced in Saskatchewan is grown under dryland conditions. During the last twenty years, common wheat production in Saskatchewan has declined by 37%, while the durum wheat area has increased by 13% as a result of hefty subsidies for wheat production and export enhancement in the EU and USA. Canada's freight railway industry moves more than CA$280 billion worth of goods from coast to coast. Rail shipping has been highly scrutinized in Saskatchewan for failing to effectively get agricultural shipments to market. Record crop yields and bad weather have presented major obstacles for rail shippers. Grain elevator infrastructure in western Canada has come a long way from wood crib elevators and loading boxcars, with a flurry of activity in new elevator construction. Saskatchewan will remain heavily dependent on rail infrastructure into the foreseeable future.

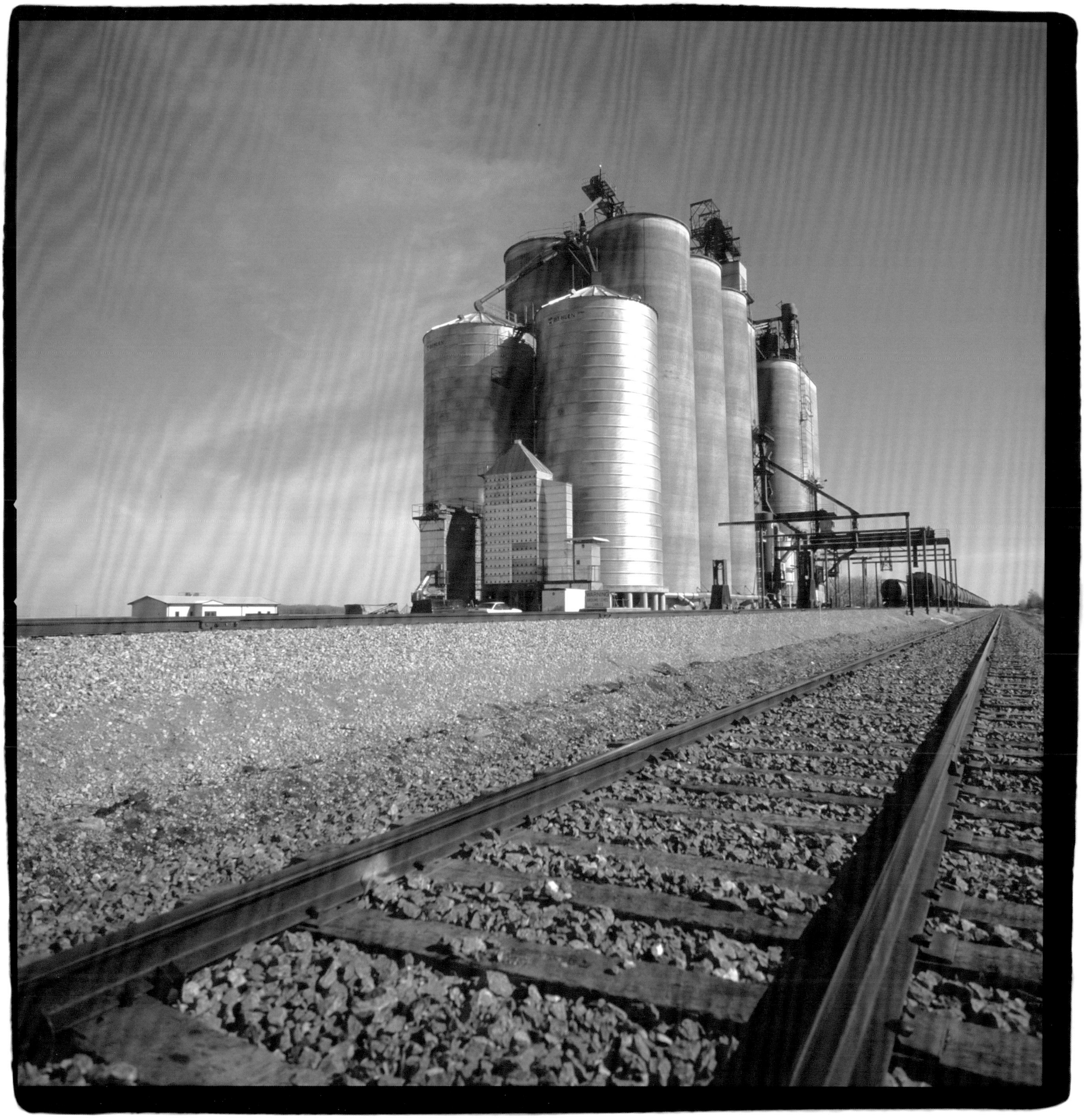

DEPTH GAUGE ON TANKER

Bayonne, New Jersey
1999

The need for oil tankers arose due to heterogeneous distribution needs of natural oil reserves and liquid chemicals around the globe. There are two basic types of oil tankers: crude tankers and product tankers. Crude tankers move large quantities of unrefined crude oil from the point of extraction to refineries. The main deck of an oil tanker is mounted with a network of pipelines used to load and unload cargo oil to and from the ship. The size of oil tankers saw a rapid increase in the mid-1970s due to abundance in global oil consumption and trade. Due to the skyrocketing of oil prices, the quantity of oil being traded by sea has considerably reduced, and few new ultra-large and large crude carriers have been commissioned. Water depth markings on the bow of a steel ship indicate the weight of the contents. The depth of the ship is measured as the distance between the undersides of the deck amidship to the bottom of the keel.

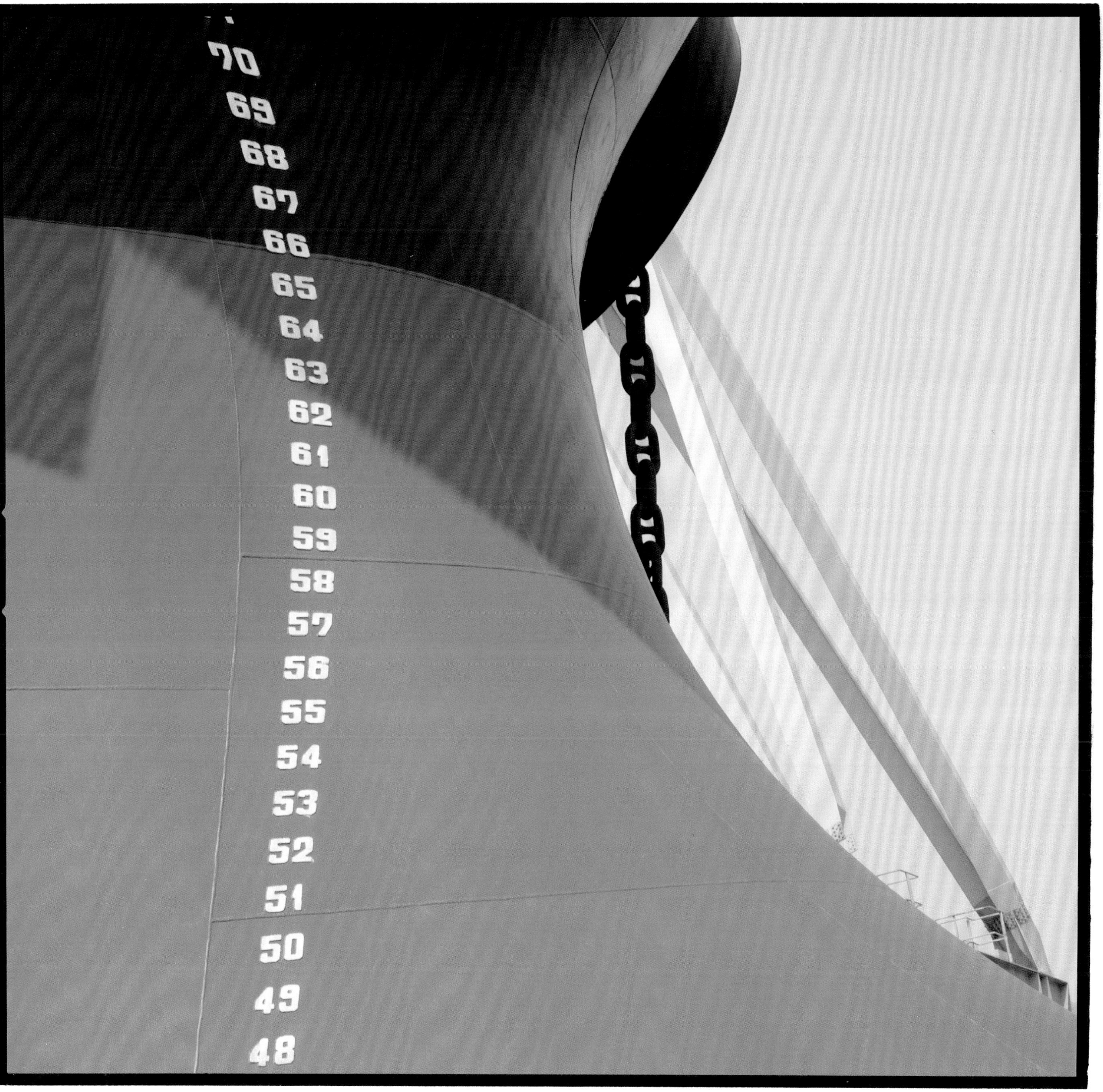
70
69
68
67
66
65
64
63
62
61
60
59
58
57
56
55
54
53
52
51
50
49
48

PANAMA CANAL

Third Set of Locks,
Panama City, Panama
2015

The Panama Canal expansion project begun in 2007, called the Third Set of Locks Project, doubled the capacity of the Panama Canal by adding a new lane of traffic for larger ships. The new ships, New Panamax, carry twice as much cargo. The design built two new lock complexes—one each on the Pacific and Atlantic ends of the canal. Each new lock complex is composed of a three-lift lock, with three water-saving basins per lift chamber, as well as a redundant closure system of eight rolling gates. The new locks have water-saving basins to reduce the volume of water that is needed in lock operation. The new lock chambers are 180 feet wide compared with the old canals at 110 feet; 1,400 feet long compared with the old at 110 feet long; and 60 feet deep compared with the old at 41.2 feet deep. With the third set of locks, the canal will be able to manage the traffic demand forecast beyond 2025; total inflation-adjusted revenues for that year are predicted to amount to over US$6.2 billion. Completion was slated for August 2014, to coincide with the 100th anniversary of the opening of the Panama Canal, but various setbacks and strikes by the Spanish contractor that grossly underbid pushed back the completion by two years. Due to a restrictive contract, contractors were not compensated for the cost overruns and stopped construction in retaliation. Eventually, US$1 billion additional funding was provided from other sources. Total construction cost was US$5.25 billion. Commercial operation of the expanded canal began on June 26, 2016. Total inflation-adjusted revenues for that year exceeded US$6.2 billion.

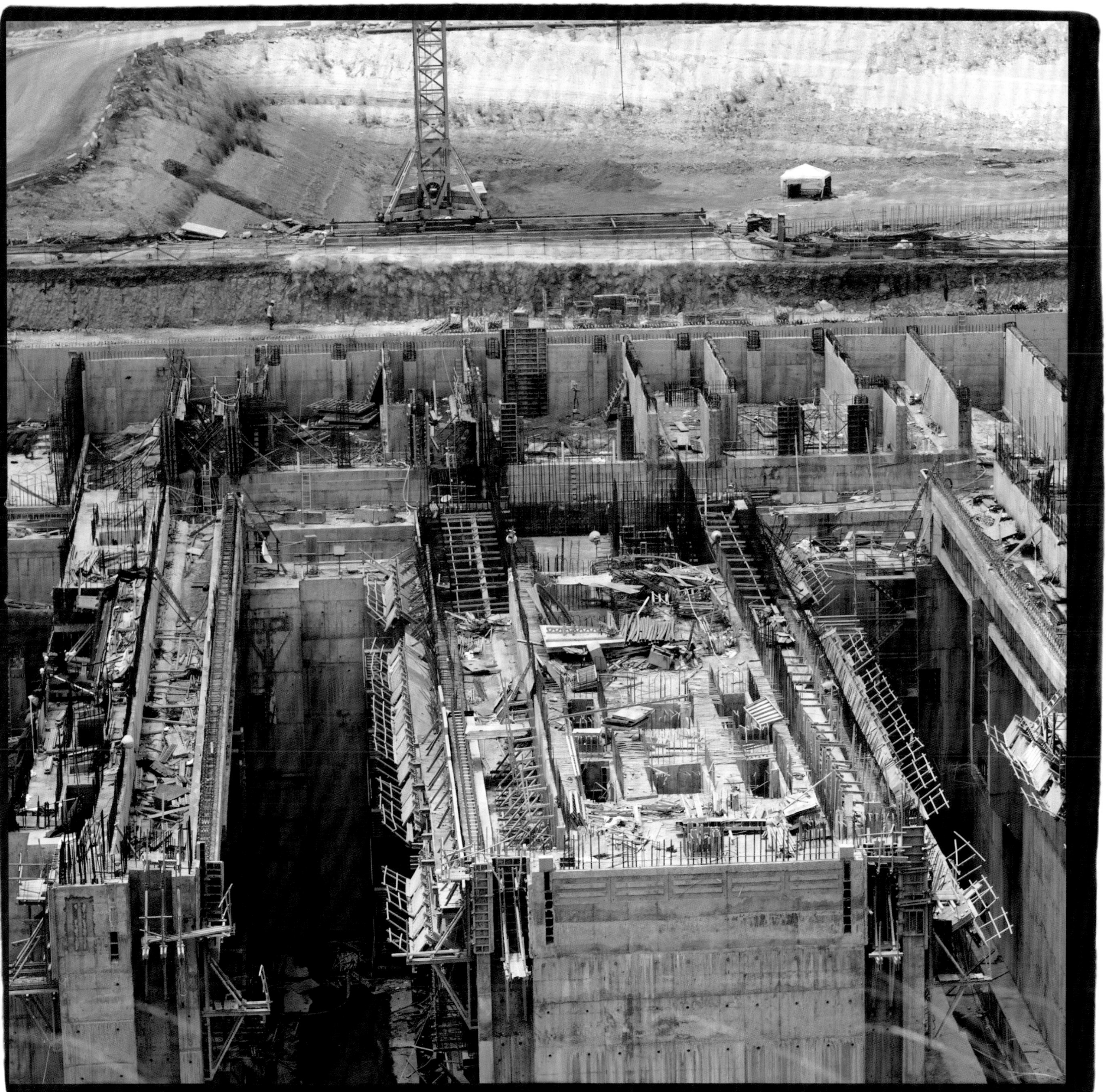

LIVORNO SHIPYARD PROPELLER

Livorno, Camp Darby, Italy
1981

In the years following the Axis powers' surrender and the close of World War II, Italy and the United States signed a treaty that allowed for the United States to occupy a section of land near Livorno, and in 1951, Camp Darby was established. It is currently under Italian military control and is managed by Italian authorities. Camp Darby is named in memory of Brigadier General William O. Darby, who was killed in 1945 by enemy artillery. It is home to the only US military beach in Europe, American Beach, popular with US military personnel across Europe. Camp Darby has historically been home to a wide range of United States military units. Located on the same property is the Accademia Navale, inaugurated on November 6, 1881, as the union of the *"Regia scuola di marina"* in the Kingdom of Sardinia, and the "Borbonica" following the unification of Italy. The US military base houses 100 men with the 731st Munitions Squadron. The Italians use Camp Darby to house the headquarters of a special operations regiment and a support battalion. This photograph was shot outside the historic walls where shipbuilding took place.

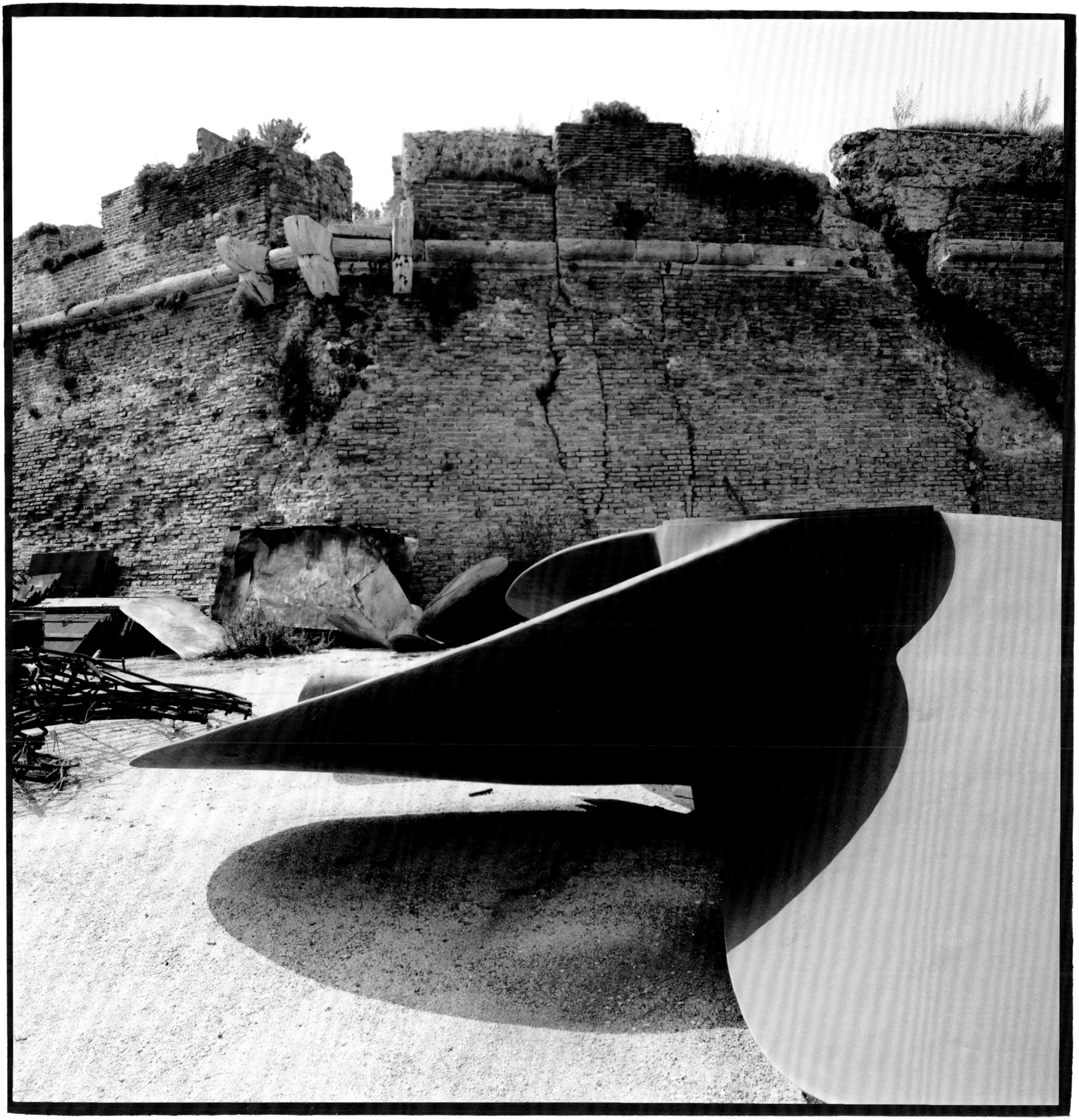

FUTURE

CERN-ATLAS

Geneva, Switzerland
2014

The European Organization for Nuclear Research is known as CERN. CERN's main function is high-energy physics research. The Large Hadron Collider (LHC) is the world's largest and highest-energy particle collider and the largest machine in the world. It was activated on September 10, 2008. The LHC consists of a 16.78-mile ring, 164 to 574 feet underground, of superconducting magnets with a number of accelerating structures to boost the energy of the particles along the way. Inside the accelerator, two high-energy particle beams travel at close to the speed of light before they are made to collide in two ultrahigh vacuum tubes. Particles are guided around the accelerator ring by a strong magnetic field maintained by superconducting electromagnets. ATLAS is one of two general-purpose detectors at the LHC. It investigates a wide range of physics including research into dark matter. Beams of particles from the LHC collide at the center of the ATLAS detector making collision debris in the form of new particles. Six different detecting subsystems arranged in layers around the collision point record the paths, momentum, and energy of the particles, allowing them to be individually identified. The interactions in the ATLAS detectors create an enormous flow of data. To digest the data, ATLAS uses an advanced "trigger" system to tell the detector which events to record and which to ignore. ATLAS is 46m long, 25m high, and 25m wide; weighs 7,000 tons; and is the largest-volume particle detector ever constructed. The important discovery of the Higgs boson by ATLAS and CMS detectors was a breakthrough. It transforms (or "decays") into lighter particles almost immediately after being produced and is the particle that gives all other fundamental particles mass. The Higgs boson could hold clues as to the nature of dark-matter particles, which comprise 95% of our universe. I shot this photo for *The New York Times* after traveling from Turkey on Christmas Eve. It was taken 1,000 feet underground at the CERN facility in Switzerland.

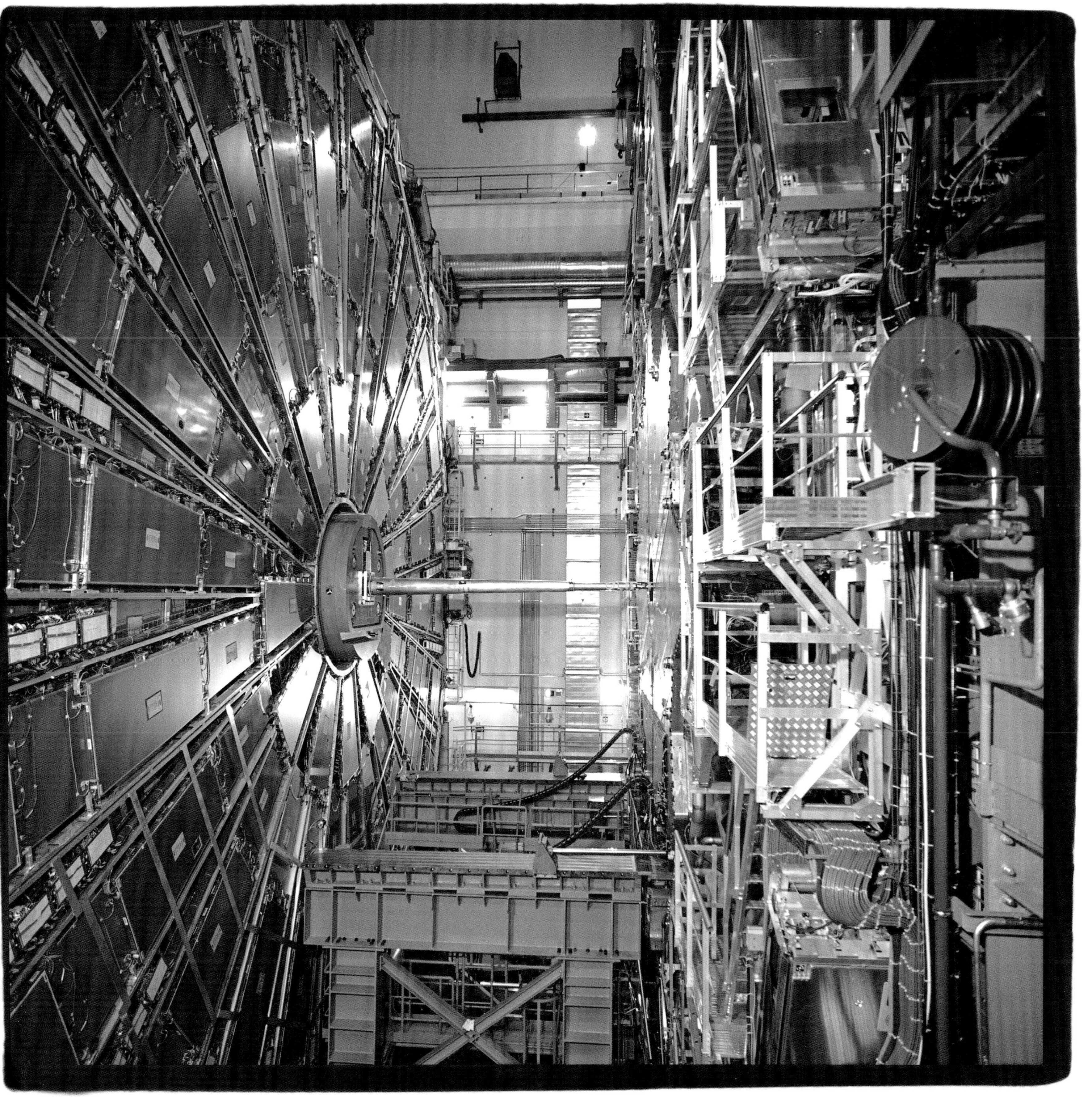

GLOBAL HAWK

Northrop Grumman RQ-4,
Mojave Desert, California
2015

The Northrop Grumman RQ-4 Global Hawk is a high-altitude, intelligence-gathering, 12,300-nautical-mile range, remotely piloted surveillance aircraft designed by Ryan Aeronautical (now part of Northrop Grumman). In active operation with the US Air Force since 2001, Global Hawk sees potential threats to allow commanders to gain greater understanding of an area of interest. It can survey as much as 40,000 square miles (100,000 km2) of terrain in a day, an area the size of Iceland. These same intelligence-gathering capabilities also allow civil authorities greater ability to respond to natural disasters, conduct search-and-rescue operations, and gather weather and atmospheric data to help forecasters predict the paths of storms.
The RQ-4 provides a broad overview and systematic surveillance using high-resolution synthetic aperture radar (SAR) and long-range electro-optical/infrared (EO/IR) sensors with long loiter times over target areas. Global Hawk is designed to gather near-real-time, high-resolution imagery of large areas of land in all types of weather—day or night. Global Hawk has amassed more than 250,000 flight hours with missions flown in support of military operations in Iraq, Afghanistan, North Africa, and the greater Asia-Pacific region.

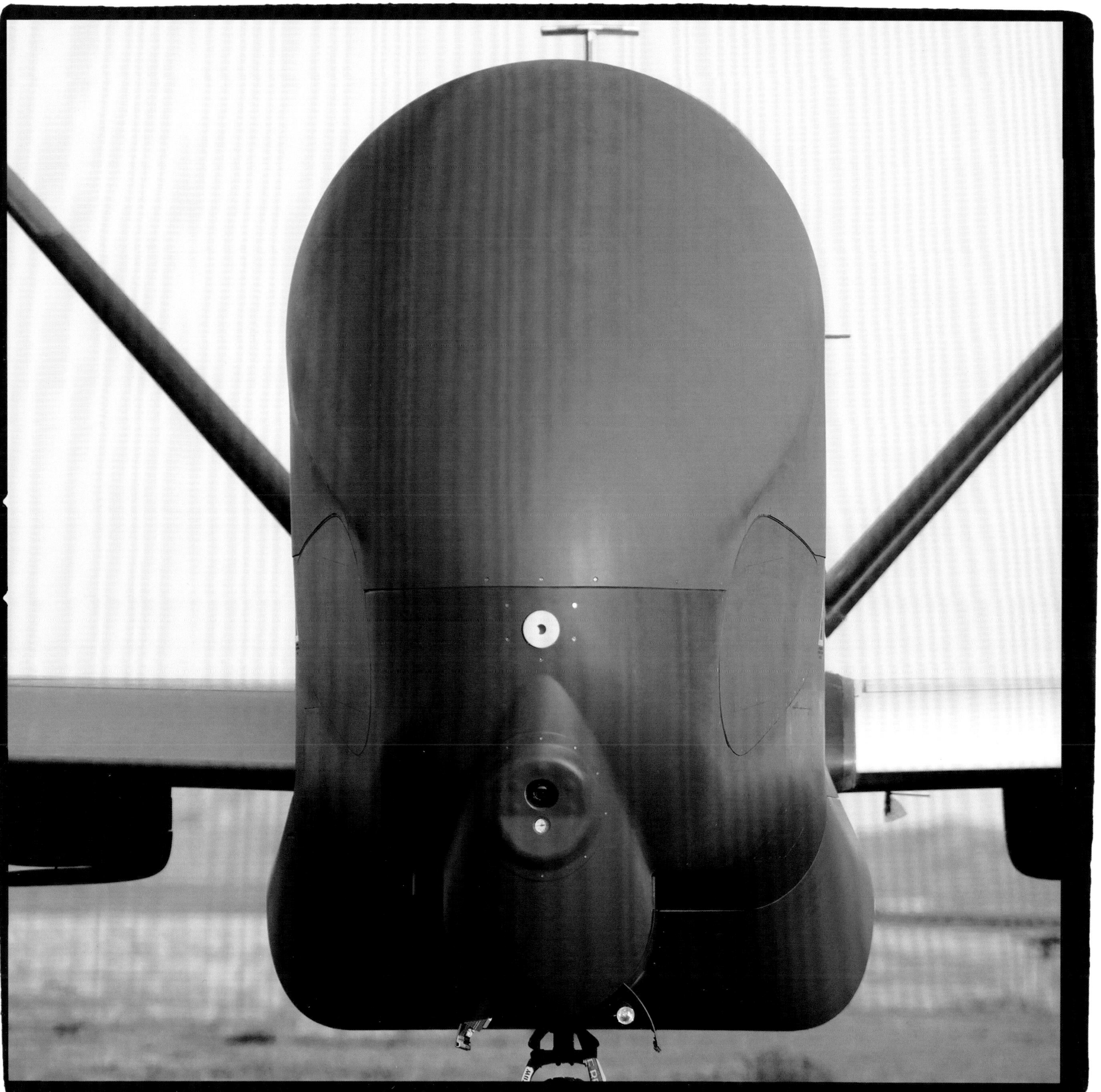

EKSO BIONICS

Exoskeletons,
Oakland, California
2014

Ekso Bionics Holdings, Inc., develops and manufactures powered exoskeleton bionic devices that can be strapped on as wearable robots to enhance the strength, mobility, and endurance of soldiers and paraplegics, improving quality of life. These robots enable individuals with any amount of lower extremity weakness, including those who are paralyzed, to stand up and walk. The company's first commercially available product is Ekso. Ekso weighs 45 pounds, has a maximum speed of 2 mph, and a battery life of six hours. The exoskeleton was originally designed to assist military veterans who have been paralyzed in battle. Another use case is enhancing the ability of soldiers to bodily transport heavy equipment. Ekso Bionics is also the developer of HULC, now under military development by Lockheed Martin. EksoNR is another Ekso invention, a robotic exoskeleton specifically designed to be used in a rehabilitation setting to progress neuro rehabilitation patients so they can walk out of therapy with the device and back into their communities. As the first exoskeleton FDA-cleared for acquired brain injury, stroke, and spinal cord injury, EksoNR assists in re-teaching the brain and muscles how to walk again.

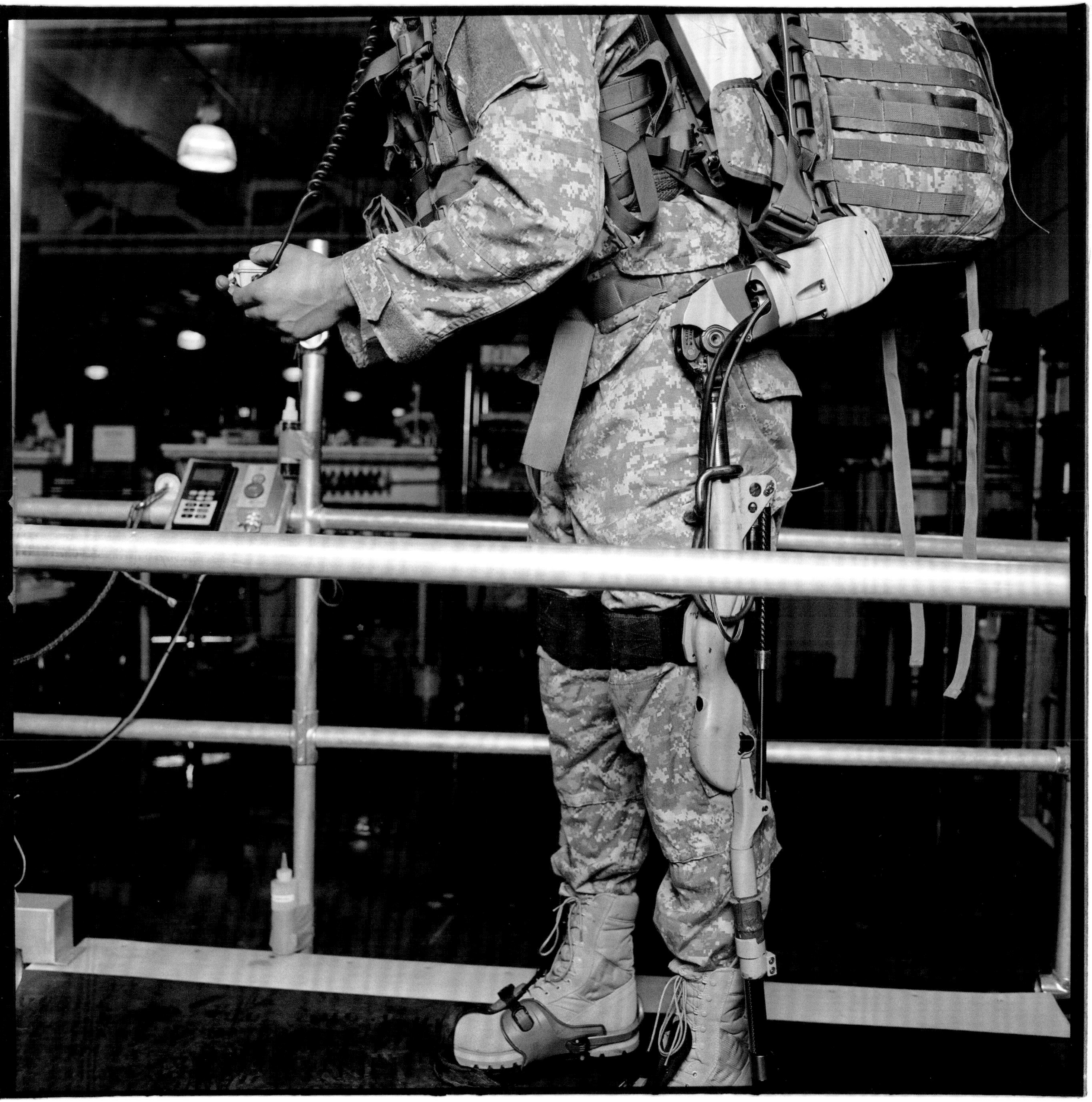

SCRIPPS MEDICAL CENTER

Radiosurgery NMR,
San Diego, California
2017

Kurt Wüthrich, from the Department of Molecular Biology at the Scripps Research Institute, won the 2002 Nobel Prize in Chemistry for "his development of nuclear magnetic resonance spectroscopy for determining the three-dimensional structure of biological macromolecules in solution." Magnetic resonance imaging (MRI) is a procedure used to help diagnose a wide variety of conditions. The MRI scanner uses a powerful magnet, radio waves, and computer technology to produce pictures of internal body structures from all angles—without ionizing radiation. MRI medicine fostered a new field, radiosurgery. "CyberKnife" stereotactic radiosurgery at Scripps Clinic Radiation Therapy Center is ideal for brain tumors. The patient lies on a table and a robotic arm, controlled by a computer, moves the radiation linear accelerator, focusing radiation exactly on the area being treated with sub-millimeter accuracy. This NMR device weighs more than a 737 aircraft. It rotates around the patient's brain tumor, minimizing the damage to the surrounding tissues, to reduce the tumor size with lasers. A continuous beam would create damage to the brain, but the circular pattern deflects this continuous bombardment of beams.

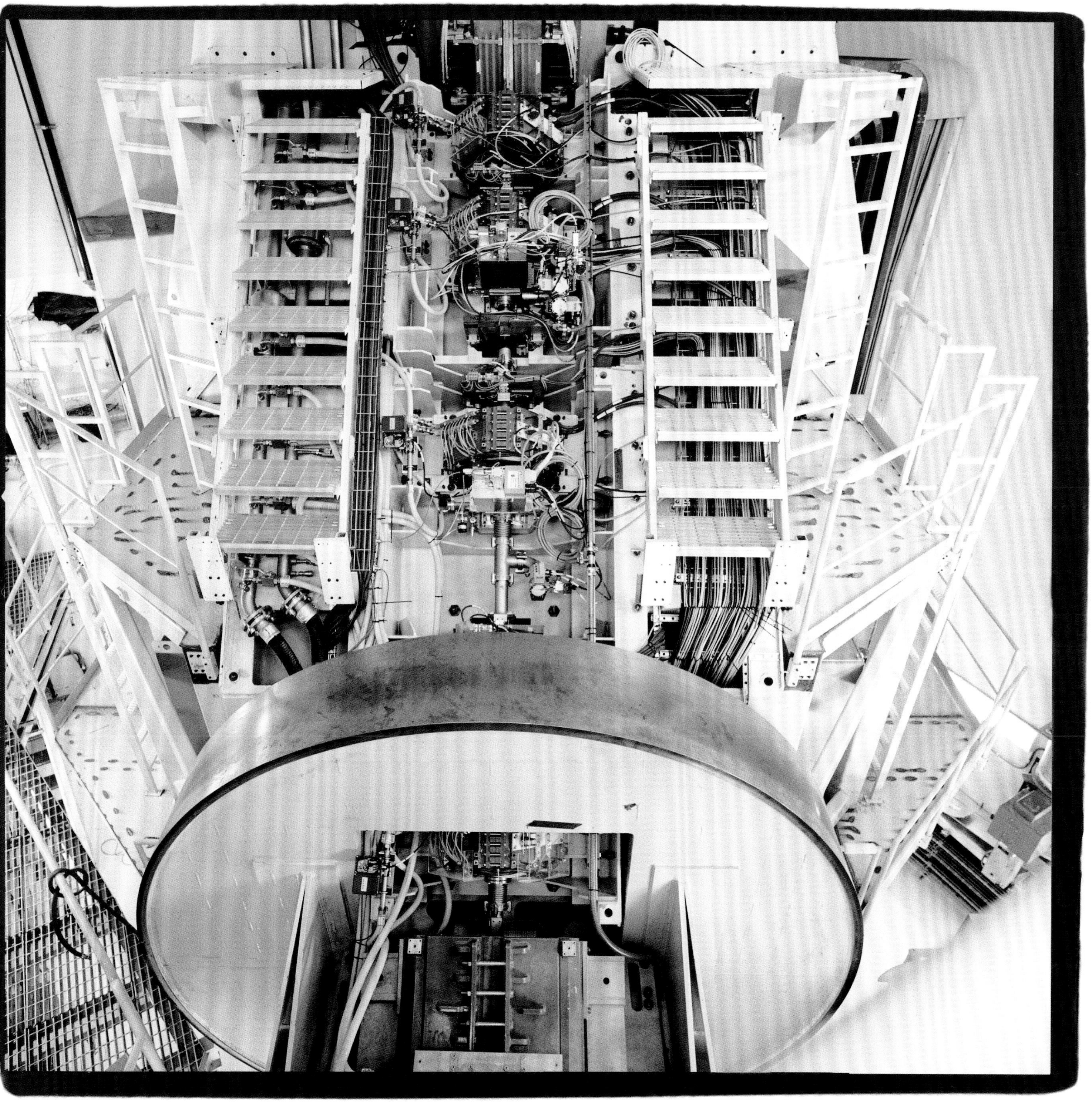

META SERVER FARM

Prineville, Oregon
2017

Meta's hunger for new data center capacity is fueled by the outsize role video now plays on its platform: live video, 360-degree photos, virtual and augmented reality. Meta is one of several companies in the world considered to be hyper-scale data center operators. Along with Amazon, Alphabet, Microsoft, Alibaba, Tencent, and Baidu, this group operates the world's largest cloud platforms, designed from the ground up to serve customers at global scale. This building's ultimate total footprint will be 900,000 square feet. Meta has invested more than US$1 billion to build its Prineville campus (two new buildings are in construction now), which currently consists of two full-fledged data centers and a cold storage facility. The first corporate data center opened in Prineville in 2011. When complete in 2023, the nine-building campus will consist of nearly 4 million square feet, equivalent to 24 Costco stores, dropped on the edge of a small Oregon town with about 10,000 residents. Data centers are not major employers, with just a few hundred people working at Meta's enormous Prineville facilities, but they provide an infusion of construction jobs. The electricity used by the data centers generates US$2 million in franchise fees. Energy consumption expectations for the cloud computing industry have been projected to consume as much as 5% of the US's annual electrical power production in coming years.

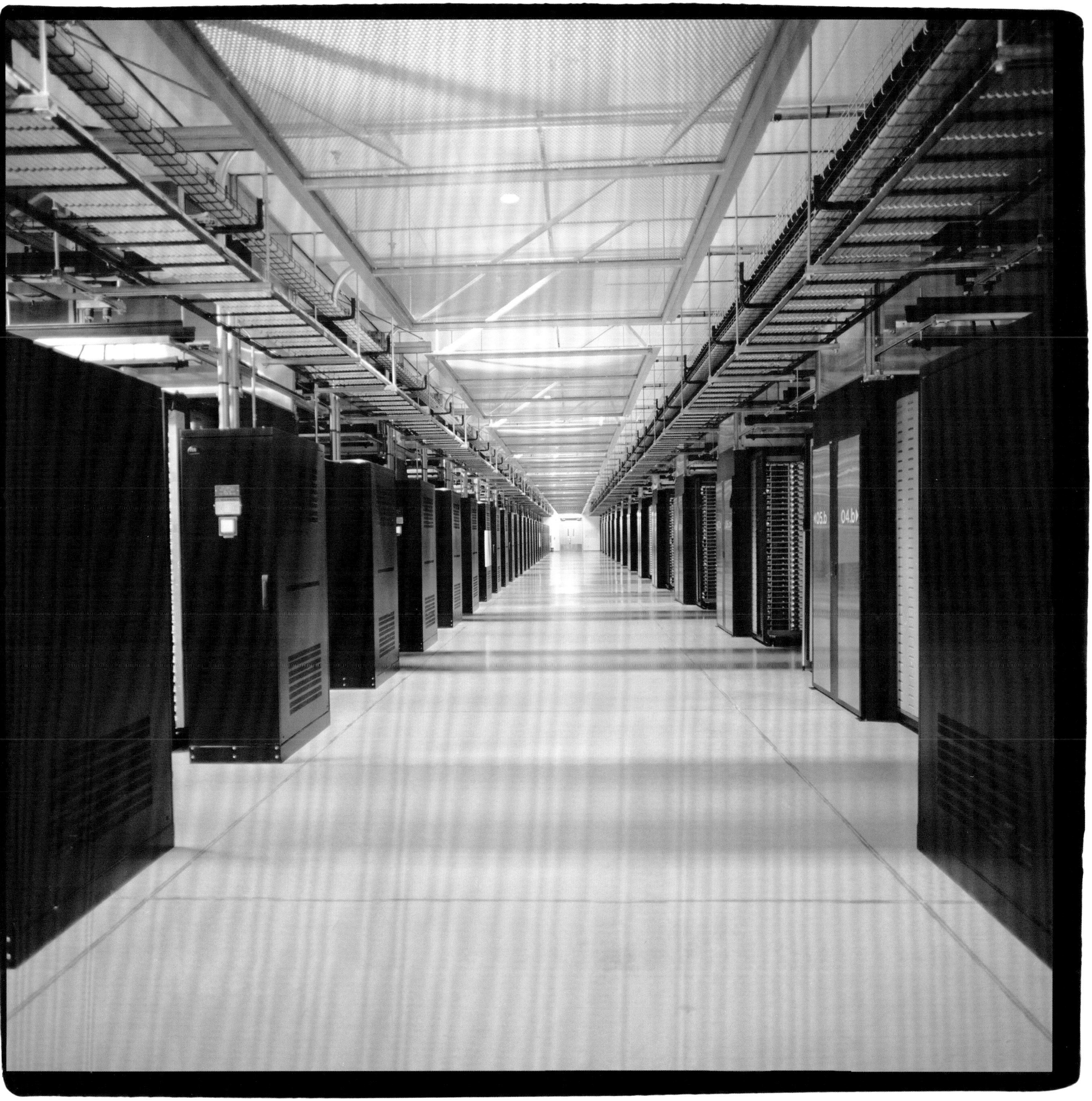

SALK INSTITUTE

La Jolla, California
2017

Jonas Salk was a miracle worker who never patented the polio vaccine he discovered in 1955, or earned any money from his discovery; Salk preferred it be distributed as widely as possible and spent his last years searching for an HIV vaccine. He passed away in 1995. His life's philosophy is memorialized at the Salk Institute: "Hope lies in dreams, in imagination, and in the courage of those who dare to make dreams into reality." Louis Kahn, the famed architect, designed the Institute's buildings. The Institute opened in 1965. One stroke of architectural genius, which allows for the Institute's remarkable flexibility, was the physical design of the floors—separating lab spaces and offices from floors that contained utilities. Another unique feature is the flexible window wall assemblies. The Institute, on the edge of the Pacific Ocean, is still considered one of Louis Kahn's greatest masterpieces, "a temple to nature and a monument to scientific thought." Lawrence Halprin, the landscape architect, struggled with Kahn's vision but ultimately succeeded. The final design includes a peaceful stream running through its concourse and draining to the ocean. The Salk Institute's award-winning scientists explore the very foundations of life, seeking new understandings in neuroscience, genetics, immunology, and plant biology, and continue to foster innovation and acclaim today. "In the Salk Institute, the concrete has an enormous warmth to it, and changes in beautiful ways as the sun moves around or the fog rolls in," is an apt tribute from Nathaniel Kahn, son of Louis Kahn.

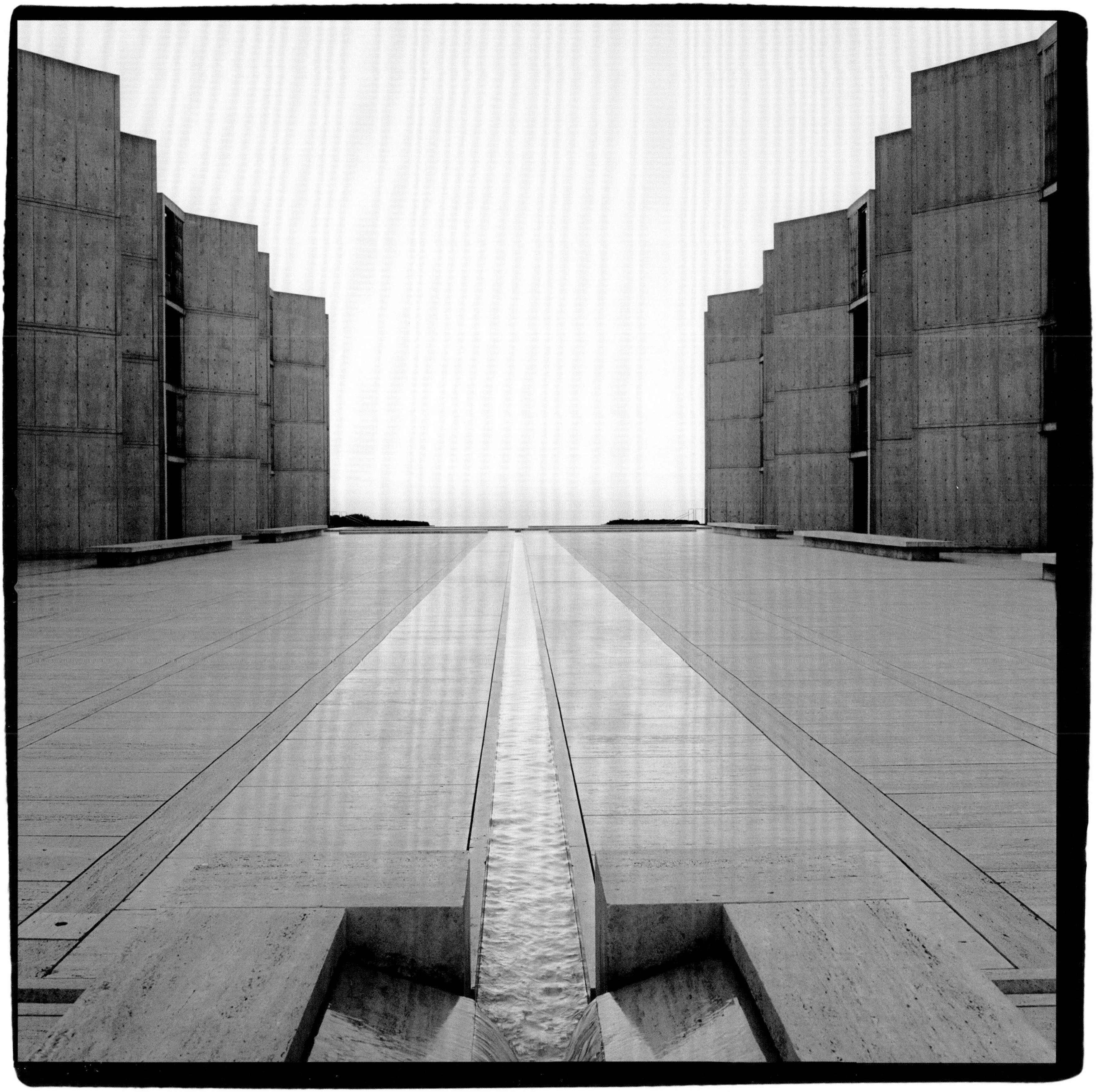

Goff Books
Published by Goff Books. An Imprint of ORO Editions
Gordon Goff: Publisher

www.goffbooks.com
info@goffbooks.com

Text by Kim Steele and Sally Steele
Photography by Kim Steele
Managing Editor: Jake Anderson

Book Design by Pablo Mandel and Kim Steele
www.CircularStudio.com
Typeset in Bau

10 9 8 7 6 5 4 3 2 1 First Edition

ISBN: 978-1-951541-15-6

Color Separations and Printing: ORO Group Ltd.
Printed in China.

Goff Books makes a continuous effort to minimize the overall carbon footprint of its publications. As part of this goal, Goff Books, in association with Global ReLeaf, arranges to plant trees to replace those used in the manufacturing of the paper produced for its books. Global ReLeaf is an international campaign run by American Forests, one of the world's oldest nonprofit conservation organizations. Global ReLeaf is American Forests' education and action program that helps individuals, organizations, agencies, and corporations improve the local and global environment by planting and caring for trees.